SCHOOLS COUNCIL

Pterodactyls and old lace

MUSEUMS IN EDUCATION

EVANS/METHUEN EDUCATIONAL

First published 1972 for the Schools Council
by Evans Brothers Limited
Montague House, Russell Square, London WC1B 5BX
and Methuen Educational Limited
11 New Fetter Lane, London EC4P 4EE

Distributed in the US by Citation Press
Scholastic Magazines Inc., 50 West 44th Street
New York, NY 10036

© Schools Council Publications 1972

SBN 423 49620 4

Printed in Great Britain by
Fletcher & Son Ltd, Norwich

PTERODACTYLS AND OLD LACE

Prow of Viking ship

Contents

ACKNOWLEDGEMENTS

Acknowledgement is made to the teachers, museum education officers and others who have contributed their views and accounts of their experiences in this field, and made available examples of children's work.

Acknowledgement is also made to the following sources for quoted material: p. 9: 'Using our museums' by Richard Cobett [Henry Pluckrose], *Art and Craft in Education*, No. 137 (June 1969); pp. 15–16: *The Sacred Grove: Essays on Museums* by Dillon Ripley (Simon & Schuster, New York, 1969 and Gollancz, 1970); pp. 25 and 26: 'The museums and the school curriculum' by Charity James in Proceedings of the First International Conference on Education and Museums, 1968 (ICOM, Paris, 1969), also published in *Ideas*, No. 11/12 (February 1969), journal of the Curriculum Laboratory, Goldsmiths' College, University of London; p. 60: 'Travellers' trophies' by G. Brett, *The Times*, 12 January 1971; p. 61: 'Should a museum be active?' by E. H. Gombrich, *Museum*, Vol. XXI, No. 1, 1968, Unesco; p. 63: 'Museums and the teaching of history' by John Hale, *Museum*, Vol. XXI, No. 1, 1968, Unesco; p. 73: 'The aesthetic education of children in the museum' by E. Larionova, *Museum*, Vol. XXI, No. 1, 1968, Unesco; p. 78: *Out of School Science Activities for Young People* by R. A. Stevens (Unesco, 1969); p. 81: 'Martinis with the Bellinis' by Roy Strong, *Sunday Times*, 26 July 1970.

Acknowledgement is made to the following for illustrations: Trustees of the Wallace Collection (p. 8); Horniman Museum (p. 12, and top right and bottom left p. 13); Science Museum (top left p. 13 and p. 32); Institute of Geological Sciences (Geological Survey photograph, Crown Copyright) (bottom right p. 13); Terry Shone (pp. 20 and 23; and p. 55 – from Birmingham City Museum and Art Gallery); Eddie Price (p. 29); Dick Chapman and Jackie Collins (pp. 42–3, 44, 46–7); Henry Grant (p. 57); Simon Farrell (p. 66); Trustees of the British Museum (facing title page, pp. 88–9, 90).

Design by Elizabeth Ryall

Foreword

This report has been written by a working party set up jointly in 1968 by the Schools Council and the Committee for Education in Museums which represents the International Council of Museums (ICOM) Committee for Education and Cultural Action in the UK.

The working party's terms of reference were to consider ways in which the services provided by museums, both national and local, could be more effectively exploited by teachers and to prepare a publication containing a clear statement of the philosophy of the educational use of museums.

Members of the working party were also asked to include in their final report some reference to the benefits derived by pupils and teachers from museum visits and loan services in terms of involvement in the curriculum.

This report could not have been prepared without the help of many teachers, students, and educationists and the working party is grateful for their stimulating and often provocative contributions, many of which appear in this report.

The working party has not sought to present a list of conclusive findings, but rather to describe many ways in which museum resources are currently being used by teachers and other educationists. Problems are posed and discussed but are left open-ended to emphasize the need for further study and active investigation. The aim has been to draw attention to the enormous museum potential, to make known what is being done already, and so to provoke comparison and to encourage fresh experiment and new methods of work.

Rubens' The Rainbow Landscape

Chapter one

Forward looking

There were one or two small groups enthusiastically studying period rooms but there were also large parties which were doing the collection crocodile-fashion. This consists of a senior teacher proceeding in front at a measured tread around the edge of the galleries without pause, or as much as a glance to left or right. The children follow, two by two behind. The column moves inexorably towards the exit, home time and tellie. One wonders again what is the point of this type of operation. As a demonstration of class control it is masterly. The visit can be recorded in the headteacher's log and after all the children can buy postcards and booklets as they leave and write a piece about it. But again I would ask, does it really give children the experience that they need – to go, to see, to feel, to recapture, to relive? For it is from an amalgam of these experiences that understanding will come and with it something of that appreciation of our culture. It is this surely that we should look for in visiting a museum. (Richard Cobett 'Using our museums')

This comment was made by a teacher after watching a group of children being led around a museum. Such a practice, once in general use, is now seen less frequently. Today, we take it more for granted that children should not be led around the galleries crocodile-fashion, thirty or forty strong, but rather that they should work individually or in small groups. We assume that they come not merely to listen to a teacher or to a museum expert, but to enjoy the objects, to learn how to look at them, and, through looking, to distinguish differences in styles and in textures, to perceive similarities and patterns. Visiting a museum in this way can be exciting. It has an element of personal discovery which helps to involve children and make them feel at ease. It is not just a matter of getting them to list information, however, or to answer questions, but of providing them with opportunities for first-hand experience so that gradually they come to observe and to select, to recognize traits that are typical of certain periods, for example, or to spot characteristics of certain rocks, shells, or insects. Names, dates, factual information and explanations are important, but they follow later and, because they then relate to what has been seen and understood, they become more meaningful in a way otherwise impossible, and are consequently remembered.

Encouragement of this visual approach to learning is the special contribution that the museum can make to education. It goes with open-ended methods of work and, even though the class may all be studying the same theme in the same gallery, it allows each child a personal response to a particular exhibit. This response will be partly aesthetic and partly the result of curiosity, and it will involve associations that differ from individual to individual. The visual approach to learning provides a basis for further development in the classroom and avoids many of the psychological difficulties often aroused when children visiting a museum come face to face with rows of glass cases or the admonition 'don't touch'. Learning visually to analyse and to recognize can so involve the child that these frustrations lessen and gradually disappear. He forgets the first forbidding impression that the museum may have made. If this visual involvement is followed by the handling of exhibits set aside for the purpose, either in the museum or in the school, the handling itself becomes more significant because it is related to previous visual experience.

The enclosing classroom is becoming obsolete; the scope of the school has widened beyond its walls. Children develop in a broader environment; the surrounding world serves their schooling. Children of all ages are encouraged to explore, to make choices that are personal and have meaning. What better than the museum with its great diversity of objects to provide stimulus for their activities? The objects, which range from the familiar to the unknown, are surely as much part of a child's surrounding world as are bridges, airfields, churches, and steelworks. Crystals and shells, fossils, sculpture in steel, in glass, and in cement, masks and musical instruments, compasses and sextants, exotic birds, prehistoric dinosaurs, vintage cars, and aeroplanes can be as exciting to explore as slag heaps, ponds, and farms. Forward-looking teachers will encourage children to discover and enjoy the resources of their local museums. At York there are steam engines, at Greenwich the State Barge, at Birmingham the glass prisms from Grace Darling's lighthouse, at Bath the Wild West Saloon, at Cambridge a collection of Staffordshire bears, muzzled for baiting. There is also a multiplicity of small museums where much that is amusing, improbable, and worth while waits to be discovered, museums that will give children opportunities to create out of vivid personal experience. We must remember, however, that a child's response can sometimes be so intense that communication is of no importance and the need to make or learn is overridden by an emotion that is enough in itself.

Chapter two

What is a museum?

A museum is in essence a collection of collections. The urge to collect is common to child and adult alike. It can start early in life; the contents of a boy's desk or trouser pocket is often a collection in embryo, as richly stimulating to the youthful imagination as the art gallery to the painter. In the same way, the adolescent's pleasure in expressing personal ideas and preferences shows itself in the array of objects that transform an impersonal college room. They excite the eye and stir the imagination; they are products of today and starting points for personal discovery.

This first stir of interest and pleasure can lead, when encouraged, to the more far-reaching adult understanding and enjoyment of museums. The problem is how to develop this intimate personal relationship with the impersonal array of objects in museums and galleries. Students and younger visitors may be helped by realizing these seemingly amorphous collections were, in their beginnings, as much expressions of personal preference and interest as their own, and that even now the selection, choice, and display reflect personal taste and preferences. Most museums were not originally planned for public use: more often they were private individual collections which were in time opened to the public. Today it is hard to discover a personal quality in the national collections, but it is still discernible in the smaller museums and galleries.

COLLECTION TO MUSEUM

When does a collection become a museum? There are several definitions of museums. All include acquisition and conservation in their list of functions. Some mention display and education, others include study and research. The definition given in the *Encyclopaedia Britannica* is:

Museums acquire and study objects of historic and aesthetic value which serve to illustrate certain developments and trends, and from these select objects and exhibit them in installations planned to inspire and educate the public.

This definition points out the difference between the museum and the private collection and indicates the extent of the museum's responsibility. Collection and conservation are common to both, but the museum is also called on to exhibit and so to inspire and educate. These differences in definition also show that agreement is by no means unanimous among museums as to their functions. There are those who favour the scholar rather than the general public, those who prefer selective display rather than display of quantity, those who are more concerned with aesthetics than with popular education, and those who give preference to acquisition, conservation, and research. In recent years this exclusive attitude has been greatly modified and most museums make increasing efforts to come to terms with the mounting numbers of adults and children who form their vast new public. Indeed, it is the needs of this public that have determined the general policy to promote education, to popularize, publicize, and integrate the museum more fully into everyday life. These are new and heavy demands on staff who still have to carry out their main functions of collecting and conserving. This is sometimes overlooked, and the public, especially school visitors, forget that their needs are always relative to the exhibits, which are the *raison d'être* of the museum; that identification, cataloguing, and display are essential to any subsequent activity in which they can participate.

*A Goliath beetle
from West Africa*

THE RANGE OF MUSEUM ACTIVITIES

What sort of a picture do people have of museums and galleries? Many certainly think first of the big national collections – the British Museum, the Victoria and Albert, the National Museum of Wales, etc. – all overflowing with objects both rare and excellent. Few people probably think of the great range of museums, many of them still relatively unexplored, covering almost every conceivable topic – the Mathematical Museum at Oxford, for example, or the Wellcome Museum of Medicine in London, the Museum of English Rural Life at Reading, St Fagan's Welsh Folk Museum at Cardiff, or the Pilkington Glass Museum at St Helens. Fewer still are likely to think of the museum as a developing institution, an institution that they themselves might help to start or in whose activities they might participate. And yet museums are being opened today, both nationally supported and as a result of individual enterprise, that must surely bring about a radical change in the image of the museum.

*Painted wooden mask
from British Columbia*

A miscellany of museum objects

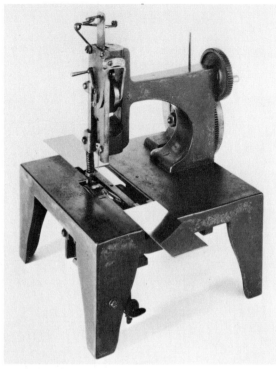

A Singer sewing machine of 1851

A sarinda from Bengal,
nineteenth century

Nineteenth-century Welsh dolls

Quartz crystals

*The Avoncroft Museum of Buildings**

Through the combined efforts of the Avoncroft Adult Residential College of Education and a group of amateurs who collaborated to save a fifteenth-century merchant's house from demolition, the Avoncroft Museum of Buildings was formed as a charitable trust and company limited by guarantee. The dismantled merchant's house is now reconstructed on the museum site in the way that it was built around 1475. The museum has ten acres of land adjoining the college and its immediate concern is to stimulate public interest in the conservation of the smaller buildings which are so often at the bottom of the list when it comes to claims on the country's limited resources.

A valuable relationship has developed with the local college of education and with primary and secondary schools. Teachers, lecturers, and children are involved in the work. A local classics master with the help of his pupils has erected an Iron Age hut and has dug pits to experiment with the storage of grain. Two young engineers have reconstructed a decayed timber windmill on the museum site; the brickwork base of the windmill was handled by boys from the local Borstal institution, who with guidance reconstructed the round house. Students from the local college of education take children to study and create at the museum, and the children enjoy it because things are actually happening there. This is a good example of co-operation between the museum and the public, and this public includes children as well as adults.

The Ripley St Thomas Museum of Agriculture and Rural Life

Sometimes developments are taking place outside the museum proper – as, for example, at the Ripley St Thomas Museum of Agriculture and Rural Life. The collection grew from a school's specific need and was made possible by the active participation of the pupils. One of the teachers at the school gives the following description of how the museum started:

The idea arose from discussions on the speed at which changes were taking place in farming and how soon a generation would be with us who knew nothing about horses and the way in which they were used on farms. Out of these discussions came the idea that some of the items passing out of use might be collected in order to have a physical record. Premises for such a collection were available, the school having taken over a small adjoining farm as a rural science unit. The buildings consisted of a shippon, calf box, and a large barn; the shippon was converted into a classroom for rural science

*See Appendix A

14

teaching, the other buildings were to be used for livestock and for the rural science unit. The barn was unsafe but with the help of the fourth-year leavers it was re-roofed to give a large display area for the items which were beginning to accumulate. Word that we were starting a collection of old farm implements spread rapidly. Children took a great interest in it and told me of things they had seen lying derelict in fields or barns. There are now offers of more items than can be dealt with for reasons which will soon become apparent.

As each item is collected attempts are made to restore it to something like its original state. This process is fairly simple with small items such as a putting-off rake or a pair of scotch hands, but a reaper which has been lying in the open for ten years presented a rather different problem and this took some six months to restore to a working condition. The children who undertake this work learn about machinery and begin to understand the development of a particular branch of farm work. It is hoped to set up a farm kitchen so that they may see how the farmer lived in the age before mechanisation.

We hope that as time goes on the museum will provide areas of interest for the woodwork and metalwork, the art and history departments and the rural science department, and that it will be a full record of historic agriculture in the Lancashire area.

The Avoncroft Museum of Buildings and the Museum of Rural Life and Agriculture at Ripley St Thomas both testify to a new attitude towards museums on the part of the public. In these instances the museum is no longer a remote place staffed by specialists to which one goes on rare occasions. It is part of everyday life. The whole community is closely concerned in its development, has a feeling of responsibility for it and, above all, enjoys it and uses it in connexion with its everyday interests.

Neighbourhood Museums

One other development that is changing the image of the museum should be mentioned – the so-called neighbourhood museum, which is an extension of the museum proper. This type of museum has close links with the community and typifies the concept of a museum without walls. The following is an account of the ambitious experiment at Anacosta, Washington DC, carried out under the auspices of the Smithsonian Institution:

One of the shapes and forms that will be designed for museums of the future must certainly be a neighbourhood museum. This concept of bringing a museum out of its setting, its museum building, is not new. A travelling exhibition is a projection of the museum itself. The school visit by a museum bus with sample exhibits is another. Museums have even pioneered the bookmobile or travelling library principle. To a large extent people from run-down neighbourhoods tend to stay there, not to be mobile or move out of their district except in the transient sense of from slum to slum. Such people referred to by a slogan phrase like 'disadvantaged' are likely never to go into any museum at all. If this is true then the only solution is to bring the museum to them. This is what we attempted to do. An unoccupied theatre was rented which by chance was in the same street as a local school and the same block as a laundromat. The seats were removed and a flat floor installed with two single steps at intervals. The exhibits resulted from a number of suggestions, primarily from the advisory council but also from the Smithsonian staff curators. A complete general store just as existed in Anacosta in 1890 occupies one corner. In it is a post office which we hope to get a licence to operate, old metal toys, a butter churn, an ice-cream maker, a coffee grinder and a water pump, all of which can work, and any number of objects of the period from kerosene lamps, flat irons, to posters and advertisements. There is another do-it-yourself area for plastic art with, at present, volunteer class instruction. There are skeletons of various kinds, some of which can be put together, some disassembled. There is space for temporary art shows, there is a TV monitor system on the stage. Occupying one of the modules is a living zoo with monkeys, a parrot, and a miscellany of animals on loan from the National Zoological Park. A great success was a shoe-box museum – an A-frame structure full of wooden shoe-boxes containing bird skins, mammal skins, shells, fossil specimens, pictures and slide projectors for extensive handling and study. A behind-the-scenes museum exhibit of leaf making, silk-screen techniques, casting and modelling, gives an additional outlet for instruction. This has incited some of them to go further afield and visit other museums.   (Dillon Ripley, *The Sacred Grove: Essays on Museums*)

Another example, 'Muse', the Bedford Lincoln Neighbourhood Centre for 'teens and adults', is run by the Brooklyn Museum of Art, and the workshops include a variety of topics: Having Fun with Words (ages 6–18), Writer's Workshop (ages 9–13), Anthropology Workshop (ages 10–14), Photography Workshop (ages 17 and above), Dance Workshop (ages 15 and above), Aviation Workshop (ages 15 and above). Here the children handle objects on loan from the museum and discuss them with responsible adults. All materials used for creative activities are free. A particular feature of this neighbourhood museum which has greatly increased its popularity is the loan service. Items can be borrowed by members and kept at home over a period of time. This is obviously an inspired way to involve the child and open the door to further activities.

These are museums of a new kind. They are as specialist in their way as some of the older institutions. The object is not only a focal point of observation but has become a means for individual activity. Traditional functions of conservation, research, and presentation are combined with this more imaginative approach. At Avoncroft as at Ripley St Thomas, at Anacosta and at 'Muse' personal involvement leads to a fuller understanding of the exhibits as well as a new awareness of the more conventional aspects of the museum's functions. To these users the collections have become identified as their collections. This points towards a new role for the museum in the community and opens wide the field for education through museums.

Chapter three

Starting points

How does the teacher who wants to introduce children to work in museums start? Obviously there are many factors to be considered and there are no infallible recipes. Here are some of the methods, however, that teachers and lecturers have used. They all stem from the recognition that a museum can offer opportunities for children to experiment and to learn through their discoveries.

A PERSONAL COLLECTION

First, a statement by a student at a college of education. This is interesting for the way in which it reveals the potential of personal collecting.

I am a hoarder. I hate throwing things away. Once something is a possession of mine, throwing it away is like losing a finger or having a haircut. I don't collect things for their value. I just come across odd objects and keep them so that they become mine. Antique collecting can be a corrupt hobby, collecting for investment and profit, or just to impress other collectors. There has to be a reason for collecting. I like the intrinsic value of bric-a-brac. My junk has got to have some tangible connexion with people. I like to know about the original owner, about the circumstances in which it was found. Like the Indian silver cigarette case taken from a dead soldier. Coins are interesting in this respect. It is fascinating to imagine what sort of pockets they have been in, whose hands they have passed through. Pipes are similar. It is interesting to imagine what the person was like who puffed down them originally. This human link becomes stronger with personal effects of relations. There is no family pride here but it is easier to picture people, to feel some connexion with the past. I possess my great-grandfather's Crimean War medals and the fact that I have a photograph of him wearing them makes the link even more real. Owning a junk collection is just one thing, but arranging it and displaying it is an art of its own. For me it is like having a mini-museum. Glass cases are sterile and as frustrating as the doors in ancient monuments or stately homes which are labelled 'not open to the general public'. This is why so many museum-goers move from one glass case to another without really taking things in. Education is the same. It is similar to learning by experience. People will know far more after picking up the junk and handling it than by passing the 'Do not touch' sign and reading the specially prepared blurb in small print in the glass case which tells them relatively nothing. Who cares about the dates of the manufacture? They are dead. Junk is still alive with ideas.

I like to arrange my odds and ends in relation to each other. Sometimes it will be according to colour or material or perhaps according to content or geographical origin. The chronological aspect is not so important since most of the objects are Victorian or early Edwardian. This age interests me and British rubbish forms the bulk of my junk with a few pieces from America and India. I feel more connexion with these. I prefer to have things I can use. Apart from obvious examples like postcards and photograph albums which are records of the past I use most of the collection in some way. I smoke the pipes, use the Indian cigarette case, the Nigerian wallet, burn joss sticks in the French perfume jar and play with the lead soldiers. I look forward to the time when I have somewhere to fill with junk and can involve myself in becoming a part, usable, of the museum.

A SCHOOL COLLECTION

Now a statement from a teacher with a school collection. One can easily imagine him as the previous student, older and more experienced, whose wish to have 'somewhere to fill with junk' has been granted:

One has to start somewhere, and since I prefer to start on my own it happened that I used what things I had. Everyone sees the need for a library of books. A library of things can be as great a stimulus and interest. It doesn't matter what things you get to start with. I sift out as I go along and parts of things may be more useful than whole objects because they start off detective work. It adds a new dimension to book illustrations when you can see patina and feel it. Things help you to separate the centuries more easily. Even old clothes provoke astute comment from very small children, particularly if robust enough to be put on. Any object in my room can be touched and handled. We use most of the Victorian kitchenware to cook in, and try out the recipes, except the ones that say 'take 40 eggs etc.' Metalwork staff often borrow forgework I have retrieved from ditches and barns and the wood-work boys turn the furniture upside-down regularly. Potters empty the cupboards when studying lips and handles and bring in sherds from the gardens.

I believe that the actual picking up and putting down of things in a random way can mean more than any formal lecture or explanation. I'm not saying the children don't need direction. We are all finding out in my room. I don't play the role of God. I'm sure it helps the children that they can see that I don't know either. Many people lend us things. We are very grateful, and we have a few dealers who come along with things they think we would like and the older children listen to the Arab-style transactions with glee.

The collection of things just grew and continues to do so. The children use almost all of it, and none is locked away. I put a careful word of instruction

Getting ready for a party. The children are polishing eighteenth-century spoons and have made cakes from old recipes, using the scales on the bench.

on the handling of things where relevant. It is a job to maintain; fourteenth-century tiles get in among the dusters and we empty our own rubbish and do our own cleaning as a safeguard. I run a dating and valuing service for parents. This way we get lots of things for a day or so. I occasionally buy something from them but am careful not to be sharp. I like to think that living among it all makes the children more selective. If they inquire why these stainless steel pans have brass bottoms they are learning some science and design. They know which is the most comfortable chair to settle in with a book. Of course we draw and paint in the usual way and sometimes we want to make the work look very desirable, associated with expensive furnishing and far removed from what one thinks of as 'school', so we find ourselves in the realm of interior decoration without realising it. We don't just put things down, we inter-arrange, thoughts between articles that have survived the centuries.

MUSEUM VISITS AND FOLLOW-UP ACTIVITIES

In contrast, another teacher who believes that visits to the museum are vital for the development of his pupils says:

I don't think that anyone can be certain what a group or individual will get from an outside school visit. The enclosed atmosphere of the school led to a realization of the need for wider experience and I felt that the pupils needed fresh sights and sounds which were unobtainable within the confines of the school.

Perhaps the most important effect the London trip had on the boys was a sudden change in their outlook on art. Before the trip art was a school subject in the school timetable, however much I tried to free them from the psychological barrier. After the trip this attitude had dramatically disappeared. Art really had nothing to do with the schoolroom at all. They had seen it could be a way of life for grown men. It was the ivories that appealed to them. I wasn't prepared for that. The minute precision was so utterly alien to anything they had done in the art department. Hardly ever had they worked on so small a scale, in so intricate and involved a manner. The attitude of 'the bigger the better' did not ring true here in the ivories cabinet.

The second visit was more profitable since I was able to point out where the various sections lay and give some anchoring advice in the hope that no time would be wasted. Side-tracking was avoided and pupils quickly gravitated to their particular interest. Unless one feels that a particular pupil ought to follow specific studies for his own good then I feel strongly that initially he is his own best intuitive guide to personal needs in the field of stimulation. I am convinced at all times it is vital never to invade, insult, or damage the privacy of the individual's right to discriminate and form opinions. He must be encouraged to move away from the shelter under which he has obtained constant guidance and sought continual reassurance. A teacher should be sensitive to this and always ready to take back as well as push out from under his wing. Development towards independence of thought and adulthood is a gradual process and may often have serious setbacks.

I am very wary about forcing influences. If I take these young potters, painters, or sculptors to places where they see different works from different periods their own values or confidence might well be knocked for six. So they ought to be firmly based on their own critical platform, confident and open-minded before being given fresh stimuli. The art gallery and the museum are good places to pick up techniques provided that the inventiveness of the pupil is not stifled and weakened.

The fourth example is from a report by the head of a remedial department of a secondary school whose pupils took part in a pilot study conducted by one of the national museums:

This school is in an area where much of the housing is substandard. Many of the pupils come from broken homes, fathers in prison and the boys often in trouble with the police. The pupils who took part in the study were 15 school leavers from the remedial stream and were by no means willing or easy to instruct. One of the main causes of their inability to read or write adequately is their lack of background knowledge and experience. 'Don't touch', 'don't ask questions', 'shut up', has stunted their growth so much that they are almost unable to receive external stimuli. In the past, museums and art galleries and parks have added their share of prohibitions to the list. It seemed to me therefore that a museum situation based on 'please pick this up', 'do examine it', 'how does it feel?', 'what is it made of?', 'what is it used for?', backed with experts willing and ready to answer questions in such a way as to raise other questions, could not but be a success with our boys.

We visited the museum with two groups, each group coming twice. The first group made a series of coloured slides of boys working in the demonstration room and linked them to a taped commentary of boys describing the object they would most like to take home with them. This proved to be very successful and boys who normally express themselves with difficulty were able to find words to say why they liked the object they had chosen; the tape helped to refresh their memories when it came to written work at school.

The second group took cameras with them and each boy was allowed three shots. He had first to choose and sketch his object. This helped him to look closely and to decide how he would photograph it.

On return to school one boy took charge of the tape recorder and another of the coloured slides. They arranged these and then invited the boys who took them to speak into the recorder. This they did willingly but often found it difficult to remember any hard facts about the objects, and when their books could not supply the information, they invented their own. Historical accuracy suffered but for my immediate purposes it was sufficient that they were thinking, using words, setting their own technical standards. They made three versions of the tape before they were satisfied, and arranged it so that the slides appeared on the screen a fraction before their description was heard on tape. It is not a masterpiece but in terms of motivation and communication between pupils and between pupils and myself the visit was a success.

A matchbox museum made by a child aged six

A different but effective use is made by groups of boys from a grammar school who spend three days at the National Maritime Museum after their O level or A level examinations. They are not necessarily boys whose first interest is history, but are volunteers who undertake to write up their findings, using printed sources to put their documentary evidence into a broader setting. They give their subject preference but are advised to accept guidance from the custodian of archives at Greenwich, for it is important in so limited a time to study something that is a manageable entity and for which useful documents are available.

We write in good time to inform the museum what the boys would like to study and get their reactions and alternative suggestions. The special merit of the National Maritime Museum for school projects is the subject matter which is intrinsically interesting to boys – naval operations, explorations, with botany, cartography, navigation, anthropology, the complex operations of ships' maintenance, and dockyards. The museum can provide varying materials and back the documents with maps, prints, paintings, and sometimes models and relics. For instance, a naval expedition can be studied in an admiral's order book, the ship's logs, a curtly illustrated personal journal or letters or in the dockyard officers' reports of fitting out and supply. Such variety is not often found in Poor Law records, etc., which students are given to wade through in local authority archives. The staff of the museum welcome and give thought to the topics and documents best suited to beginners. The school has made a small grant towards buying photographs of maps, documents, paintings to illustrate the work and many boys use their own funds.

This activity is obviously demanding on an already hard-pressed museum staff – the assembling and selection of documents, the supervising and helping of the boys in using the material suggests a case for preparing folders of reproductions or transcriptions which could be studied before going to the museum. Something on the lines of the Jackdaw series – the log book of one of Holmes' squadron, a set of orders or agreed signals, letter home, etc., could whet the appetite before studying the original charts, models or paintings. A folder on the special exhibition prepared each year by the museum staff would send a school party to the exhibition with their curiosity aroused. I do not think that children have the patience once confronted by a display to pause and read and think about the explanations attached to the exhibits, however well written.

What have these descriptions of work with children and students in and out of museums in common? In each case it is the teacher or student-teacher who has appreciated the educational potential of the museum, has not attempted to force or coerce a particular message or viewpoint, but has encouraged individual involvement and discovery, and has been there to further and deepen the personal experience when the moment is ripe. Museum education, for these teachers, is not an appendage to their teaching, but an integral part of it. They are putting into practice views expressed by an educationist who said:

The role of the teacher in this kind of work in museums is increasingly that of adviser and consultant. He will look eagerly at the true expert to play the same role but at a higher level. This change of role is in line with another development; the old didactic techniques, even the use of the assignment or questionnaire, arose out of a faith in the importance of factual knowledge. But as our world of culture explodes into vast new areas of knowledge, we are coming increasingly to believe in something we have talked of for generations and so rarely practised – the importance of learning how to learn. Gradually we are learning to practise what we have preached and are concerned to help children to acquire effective habits of investigation, to use expert evidence, to evaluate opinions, to try imaginatively to see other points of view, to perceive relationships between facts. In all these processes museum education has far more to offer than the mundane fact-collecting encouraged by some schools as often suggested in the past. (Charity James, 'The museums and the school curriculum')

Chapter four

Learning and teaching

Today, when education is freeing itself from traditional didactic techniques, when our concern is to help children to acquire habits of investigation, to perceive a relationship between facts and objects, the museum has a unique contribution to make. It is the perfect open-ended learning situation, and schools and colleges should look at it as the ideal library, laboratory, or art centre. The object, with its many facets of interest, can be a focal point for comparison, personal investigation and creative activity. (Charity James, 'The museums and the school curriculum')

But how does the teacher help children to acquire these habits of investigation? How does he help children to see, to equate an unfamiliar three-dimensional object with information they may already have, to relate what they see to descriptions given by others?

Certain techniques are at present in general use in museums: the lecture, the questionnaire or work sheet, the assignment card, the use of visual aids and special collections for handling. These have, however, too often been developed in piecemeal fashion to meet the demands of an ever-increasing number of school parties which tend to overwhelm the museum staff with requests for talks and lectures or guided tours. To what extent are these techniques compatible with the broad aims just described? It is against the background of new educational theory and in relation to the visual content of museums that they need to be reassessed.

THE LECTURE

The talk or lecture is the staple fare provided by most museums. Inevitably, however, it tends to be biased towards verbal abstractions and often fails to stimulate visual awareness or to induce personal involvement on the part of the child. At one time teachers did most of the talking in schools and the children were expected to listen and soak up information. This is no longer common practice in schools, but it still happens in the museum when the education officer gives an introductory talk or takes a group around the gallery with the children in a passive role. Interest quickly evaporates as objects they cannot see are described in language they often cannot understand.

When, however, the introduction is carefully related to the needs of a particular group and is aimed at stimulating and encouraging their involvement and participation, it can be of great value. This is the way in which one education officer introduced his subject to a group of bored girl school-leavers who were studying the Victorian period. He was brief and to the point:

If you had been pregnant a hundred years ago, you would have made baby clothes like these. And if, a few months later, you were in a difficult labour these are the instruments the doctor would have used to effect the birth – without an anaesthetic.

This startled them. They approached the exhibits that had been specially prepared for them with awe. The education officer stood by, as did their teacher, both waiting for the time when they might be needed to listen, or to answer questions. Before long, the teacher was laughing at the girls' surprise about the length of baby garments, while the education officer was discussing child mortality and giving further information about the instruments used by the surgeons and doctors. It was a long time before the girls were ready to go to the main collections and look at feeding bottles, cribs, cradles, comforters, rings and rattles, and baby books. The verbal introduction had been brief; the objects had been allowed to speak for themselves. The girls were allowed to come to terms with the objects in their own way and at their own pace. Children learn as they explain to an adult what they see, what they find, why it interests them; good discussion generates ideas and gives confidence.

Nevertheless, listening to an enthusiastic expert is an experience which most children enjoy, and we must be careful, in our concern that they should be active in the learning process, not to deprive them of this pleasure. The talks need not necessarily take place in museums, however, or be given by museum staff. A number of teachers make a practice of inviting experts and collectors to their schools to talk on subjects related to a specific museum study. A farm labourer will come to talk about corn dollies, bringing his own collection and demonstrating cutting, grouping, plaiting, and twisting techniques; a young sculptor will bring his work to an infants' school before the children visit a sculpture gallery. Children who are themselves near-experts – boys and girls who lovingly collect shells or rocks or feathers – can talk about them to other children and fascinate them with their learning.

QUESTIONNAIRES

A few years ago questionnaires were all the rage. Now there are conflicting views about them and there has been criticism of the level of activity they spark off in museums and schools. Used during a first visit, a questionnaire may inhibit a child to the extent that a potentially fruitful experience becomes a treasure-hunt in which the answer is more important than learning to look at the object. Indeed, the information is often taken not from the object but from the label, and at a later date the object is not even recognized. A teacher writes:

The work reached a higher level when children were not issued with questionnaires, work sheets, etc. If this is done, there is a tendency for the children to be so concerned with filling in the sheets that a 'quiz-contest' atmosphere is generated, with children dashing from label to case without really looking. Purposeful browsing is the best attitude to encourage.

Used frequently, such devices as questionnaires become a weakening prop. They tend to encourage teachers and education officers to over-direct the work of the children and to deny them the opportunity to seek out and create their own field of study. But questionnaires also have obvious advantages; the children are active and usually enjoy themselves. As with any teaching technique, much depends upon how and when the questionnaires are given out and what form they take. Used as a starter, a good questionnaire can help to counter the feeling of being overwhelmed which may beset any child who goes to a museum for the first time.

The following material from work cards,* taken from a set designed for a group of primary-school children studying at the Avoncroft Museum shows an imaginative approach. They were left in the classroom after a visit to the museum so that each child could select his theme of inquiry. Many were solved by first-hand observation:

    1. What would you tell your father and mother if you brought them to see the house?

*See Appendix A for further examples.

*'Choose any wall of
the house. With illustrations
describe how it is constructed'*

2. Glass was very precious and would not have been used for this building.
They had a number of ways to keep out rain, wind, and snow. If you don't know what the ways were, think up some ideas yourself.
Do you think your ideas would have been better?

3. Avoncroft House is a timber-framed building. School is a framed building of a different kind. Find out how the two framework constructions work.

Later, the children prepared question cards for themselves, for their teachers, and even for the experts in the museum.

Here are some further examples from work cards* prepared for varying age groups of children studying the collection of Greek vases at the British Museum. They may help teachers to appreciate the educational potential of such collections: they relate the past to present-day interests and cater for a wide variety of activities.

Go to the London Zoo or to Regent's Park to draw water birds. Then go to the British Museum to see how Greek artists did birds on their pots. Copy some of them. Either pretend you are a Greek artist and try to interpret your birds in that idiom or comment on some Greek aspects of your own or your friends' drawings where you think you score.

Play silhouettes. Cut out any interesting things you can think of in silhouette. Use black on white or white on black. You can do crabs or a snake, a murder, a pattern or a horse galloping, a pop group, a portrait of your friend, a new fashion, a dancer, a sunflower or your dog. Anything. Then go to the British Museum and copy the best silhouettes you can find from the Greek vases.

On Greek pots:
Find a snake and draw it.
Find a bull and draw it.
Find the best horse and draw it.
Find rare and fabulous beasts and draw the most extraordinary one you discover.

Make up your own fabulous beast.

*See Appendix B for further examples.

It should be stressed, however, that these work cards are not meant for any casual group that might turn up at the museum. Some children enjoy a choice, some classes thrive on firm but lively directives, some individuals prefer to think out their own opportunities. It would be a mistake to attempt any of these activities unless sound and sensitive working relationships exist with the class. Children unaccustomed to working on their own in school will not adapt themselves immediately to the demands made by open-ended questionnaires. But those familiar with inquiry methods of learning will get sufficient stimulus to go forward under their own steam. The very fact that children do not accept the challenge means that self-instruction, deduction, and independent investigation are unfamiliar to them. New problems, persistence in difficulty and working in depth are not tackled if they are not part of school experience.

HANDLING

There is general agreement among teachers that museums should provide objects for children to handle:

Physical contact is absolutely essential, especially where objects which were made to be handled (axes, tools of all kinds, domestic equipment) are concerned, before the full mental impact of 'real' things can be released. Museums have a very significant, and very exciting, part to play in this particular sphere of education.

or:

The authenticity of the genuine article backed by the expertise of the museum staff can vividly bring to life appropriate parts of the curriculum, create the keenest interest, and stimulate the mind and the imagination to a far greater extent than other visual aids on film or tapes, which are in comparison 'secondhand'.

or:

Children respond to 'real' objects, in a way they do not respond to other things, the 'real' thing means something very special to a child. But what is a 'real' object, using the word 'real' in the same way as a child uses it, which is hard to define? It seems to mean something authentic, not a copy; an original thing made for a purpose and used for that purpose.

and a note of warning:

Many museum educationalists work not from the inherent quality of the object, but towards the object as an illustration of some specific fact or

31

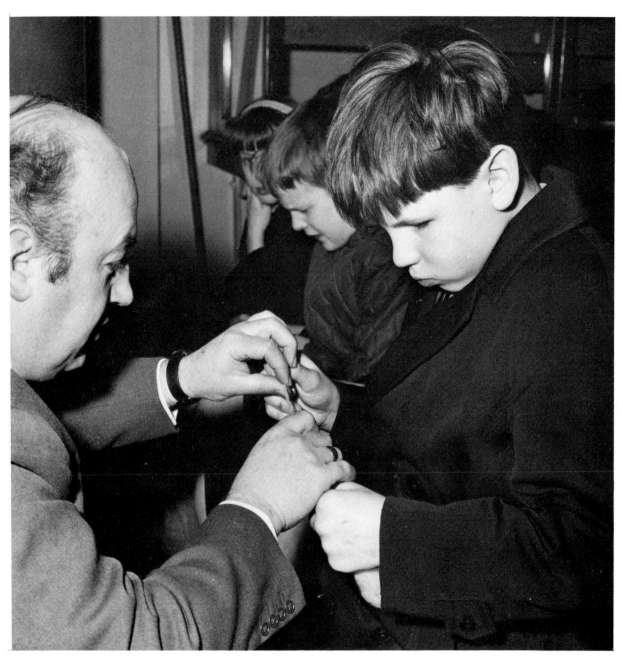

Blind children feeling yarn

theory. I believe that children should approach objects directly, through their senses (sight, touch, sound, smell) so that they can begin to discover something of their nature. This exploration, which is sparked off by direct response to the object, should encourage the child to question, study, and discover more, not only about the object itself, but by extending further to associated areas of history, biology, sociology, etc.

This emphasis on 'real' things and on the value of giving children experience of them applies generally in education. The museum, however, is in the unique position of possessing large numbers of things that are real and valuable, and it is understandable that teachers should turn to it for help. Many museums are meeting the demand by means of a loan service, or by the provision of special collections to be handled on the premises. Handling any authentic exhibit is a privilege, however, and it is for the teacher and the museum educationist to help children to appreciate that many exhibits have unique qualities which could be harmed if handled or exposed. Children respond to this sense of an object's value and are able to become involved visually when it is not possible to use tactile methods. But it must also be stressed that they do not become automatically involved with exhibits just because they are handling them. They have, on the contrary, to be encouraged to investigate, to find out by comparing weight or texture. They have to learn how to handle so as to acquire greater insight and more acute perception of qualities inherent in the object. They are capable of appreciating and responding to the expertise with which they see the specialist look at, handle, examine and assess objects of different kinds. They too can learn to recognize and to differentiate between the shapes and ornament, the quality of flints, metals, alabaster, or marble. Awareness of this kind develops a new sensibility which extends to other activities. Learning to look is a first step towards learning how to describe what has been seen or touched. Indeed, it is this combination of looking, of touching, of creating in words or in other forms that makes up the total museum experience and that frequently differentiates museum teaching from teaching in the classroom. The inherent quality of an object is often hard to define. It relates to colour, to form, and to aesthetic values that affect the individual's likes and dislikes, his preference for one object rather than another, a preference that is purely personal. Personal engagement is vital in museum teaching, and handling, when fully used, has much to contribute. In the words of an education officer:

There is no doubt that handling the objects and comparing them, answering questions on colour and texture, making a personal selection, sketching and

33

discussing their choice, is absorbing and satisfying to all age groups. Sixth formers took longer than the less academically-able groups to settle to this unorthodox method of procedure and seemed to have more difficulty at the outset in committing themselves to a choice. But at the end of the first visit, spent entirely with the object, there was a relaxed atmosphere, great animation, and much individual discussion.

AUDIO-VISUAL MEDIA

Colour slides, photographs, facsimiles, and filmstrips are now in constant use and are on sale in most museums. Many teachers have their own collections. How and when should such aids be used? As an introduction to a museum visit? As part of the visit? Or as a follow-up? Should slides or other visual media be used in the course of a fifty-minute visit? Does this take away time that would be better spent in the gallery? How many slides should be shown in the course of a talk given in the school before the museum visit? Is it better to show one exhibit in detail or a series of unrelated objects?

These are some of the questions that still need investigation. Clearly, however, any use of these media is valid provided it extends and facilitates further study of the original. It is for the expert, with the help of the camera, to show the less experienced eye how to look, what to look for, how to explore a two- or three-dimensional object. Pupils may not always be able to study each original that they see in reproduction, but any teacher aware of the importance of colour tones and texture will encourage comparisons with an original whenever he can. Loan collections can be especially useful for this purpose.

The camera can be used dramatically to great effect, especially in film and television. Sometimes, however, the exuberance and skill of the producer are such that an original work of art is changed almost out of recognition. Dramatization is not in itself out of place; it has the power to catch the eye and arrest attention and can be a valid introduction to any study. Frequently, however, the child or adult who has first seen an exhibit on the screen is disappointed by the original. Most education officers have heard the comments 'I never thought it was as small as this', 'It looks quite different from what I imagined.' This is where help is required to bridge the gap between the original and the reproduction, so that the child discovers afresh for himself qualities often dazzlingly shown by the camera. It is to the enhancement of this personal experience that the visual aid should be directed.

34

Mechanical services in galleries at present include push-button sound tracks in the music gallery at the Victoria and Albert Museum, self-manipulated machinery in science museums, and recordings of bird songs and slide sequences of mating displays in natural history museums. Interesting films have also been made as introductions to the viewing of a limited number of objects in museum collections. These can be shown prior to a visit, but it is preferable to see them in the museum so that the children can then examine the originals with the help of the expert eye. This greatly facilitates contact and induces surprisingly intense personal observation.

Looking at Sculpture, a film made some years ago for the Victoria and Albert Museum, is an example of successful collaboration between a film director and a museum specialist to show people how to look at some of the objects in the sculpture collections. A film has also been made recently to introduce exhibits at the Maritime Museum, Greenwich. Films of craftsmen at work – stonemasons, silversmiths, or embroidresses – could also help to illuminate exhibits and show children how to look with more understanding.

In order to encourage further studies, the working party sponsored two short films of exhibits in a museum at Lincoln. The purpose was to find out the extent to which the camera could heighten perception and increase visual pleasure and so lead to further study and creative work. In the film *Insights* the objects are of a geological nature, such as rocks and shells. In the second film, *What Do I See?*, made in the Lincoln Museum, each of six objects is shown as an entity, unrelated except by the common, aesthetic qualities brought out by skilful use of the camera. Details of the films are given in Appendix D. These films will be available for study by teachers and colleges of education.

The use of the cassette in museums has not yet been fully explored either by the school or by the museum. Cassettes have been available to visitors for some time in many museums, often in various languages, but with little attempt as yet to meet the varying needs of different age groups or indeed to explore the potential of the medium. In most cases the tape is used to replace the guide-lecturer and in much the same way limits its function to providing factual information about exhibits in a particular gallery. No effort is made to involve the child or adult by means of questions, visual analysis, comparison, or selection, yet it would be ideally suited to this purpose and it would be a valuable exercise for school parties to make their own tape after a first visit, to be tried out on a later occasion in the gallery. A successful experiment of this kind in which the exhibits were photographed in the museum and the commentary was prepared and taped in the school is described on p. 22. Preparation of a tape gives ample opportunities for individual initiative, both in finding the required information and in putting it on tape.

There is no doubt that mechanization can intensify the study of museum exhibits by revealing and analysing some of their qualities. As in the case of other techniques, however, the contact with the real object does not follow automatically, especially in the case of younger age groups. They still require the skilful comment or selective question to relate their experience of the object on the screen to the object in the gallery.

These various media have been considered separately as a matter of convenience, but in reality they interrelate – the tactile with the visual, the visual with the auditory. It is not a matter of precedence: the word will awaken the desire to touch, touch will give rise to the spoken word, the camera will lead to new visual discovery and increase appreciation of the object itself. Together or singly their aim is to stimulate greater awareness and greater pleasure, which form the essence of a fruitful museum experience.

Chapter five

A study of metals in a primary school

Hammer! Hammer! Clink! Clink! Clink!
Work all day without any drink.
Pudding on Sunday, without any fat,
Poor old nailers can't earn that.

Having considered different approaches to museum studies, some of the problems, and the teaching resources, here is an account of work done by a primary school over a period of several months – an account which we hope will bring to life and make more vivid many of the points we have discussed.

The school is in Stourbridge, on the edge of the Black Country with its heavy metal industries. Lye, a centre of the nail-making industry, is close by and Redditch, famed for fish hooks and needles, lies a little to the south. This study of metals started with a group of children who were exploring the Stour, a small river which passes through Stourbridge on its way to the Severn at Stourport. The river was used extensively in industry, particularly the metal industries, and the children began some interesting research into the iron works upon its banks. The school decided it was on to something that, given a bit of impetus, might grow into an extensive study. Initially they invited a local industrialist to come to the school and talk to the children, and arranged a visit to the metal-work collections at the Worcestershire County Museum.

AN INDUSTRIALIST VISITS THE SCHOOL

The industrialist was born in the Black Country and was steeped in the traditions of the communities. He brought a fascinating collection of metal samples, tools, old newspapers, and faded photographs showing conditions in workshops, local characters, and backyard industry – where in living memory and in houses that the children know, the women worked in front of their furnaces stripped to the waist. His exhibits were put up in the school

37

hall, and here he mixed informally with the children, answering their questions and encouraging their observation, before talking to them as a group. Afterwards, and even during his talk, response was immediate. Questions and comments came from all sides and he handled them easily, for he was in tune with the children as he had been with their parents and their grandparents before them.

The scheme was begun and the tone set for much of the work that was to follow. Here is a sample from a child's study:

A Billys Cockhead nail was for fastening your drainpipe on to a wall and its nickname came from a man called Billy Cockhead and the top of the nail looks like a bowler hat. The pubs had to have pictures hanging outside because half the people could not read and the pictures were hung up with sign hooks. This is a sign hook and they made it. The chain makers drank a lot of ale, sometimes eight pints but it was hot and sweaty for them at their work. The nails for putting pictures in frames in the olden days were called sparrows bills. And they may even use them now for olden pictures. We use panel pins now because there are not many sparrows bills left. They are called sparrows bills because they look like it but I think they look thinner.

THE WORCESTERSHIRE COUNTY MUSEUM

This museum is housed in the north wing of the Bishop's Palace at Hartlebury. The collections are divided into three parts: 1. children and social life; 2. applied arts; and 3. crafts, industries, and professions. In all sections the museum is particularly rich in collections of metal work.

The museum's education officer stressed the importance of preliminary discussions with teachers. He wanted them to know the collections, the organization and the opportunities the museum could offer. Before ideas became fixed, possibilities were explored together. The most important point that emerged was that he was unwilling, for the best of reasons, to 'give talks' to the children. He preferred to create conditions for research in which children could think, explore, and record, encouraged and helped by their teachers.

One session, for instance, concentrated on metal wheels. A collection of old grinders, mincers, drills, vacuum-cleaners, etc., was placed in the schoolroom where the children could handle them easily. The natural reaction was, of course, to work the equipment, and the children were encouraged to analyse accurately the relationship between one wheel and another, particularly the cog wheels. It was wholly satisfactory to see how deeply the children went into their investigations and how the teacher and the museum education officer, by picking up their observations and questioning their findings, were able, in this carefully-designed situation, to promote an even greater degree of concentration and thought. After the exploratory session, the children were let loose in the main collections and here they went round discovering other examples for themselves. Some stayed to do detailed work on the complex wheel systems of bicycles, a meat spit in the kitchen, an early gramophone; others studied the whole range of cog wheels in smaller equipment found in the museum. They were working all over the museum, but with clearly defined aims and on a carefully prepared range of work.

Perhaps the most interesting development in school came in mathematics, when children studied the ratios connected with cog wheels, 3 to 1, 5 to 1, 10 to 1, and so on, leading to a range of work on ratios and on the properties of circles, circumference, areas, diameters, etc. After the practical experience the children were able to investigate much further than they had previously done.

The museum education officer prepared seven visits for the children and on each they explored a different range of metal work. Once they saw the smithy under working conditions and on another occasion they were given the catalogues for Samuel Lewis and Company, nail makers, and they checked the contents with the magnificent patterned display of real nails on the firm's advertising boards. The children became more and more self-reliant in their investigations and the teachers, as they came to know and understand the collections, were able to take most of the responsibility for the work.

In addition to the school visits, teachers were given access to the museum library and files for background information, and the museum education officer suggested books for the school to purchase, so that more prolonged study could continue there. The loan collection of this museum is particularly valuable because it reflects and supplements the main collections, promoting further extension of activities and sending pupils back with deepening interests in the more precious material housed in the museum itself.

After the preliminary visit to the museum's metal collections, the teachers decided to order working materials that would be in keeping with the rusty iron, the copper, brass, bronze, steel, and pewter. Finance was a problem as always, but was made easier because the school does not buy any expensive exercise books. If a book is wanted, the child makes it with a few sheets, stapling, clipping, or stitching them together. Much of the work is done on single sheets stored in individual and group folders and can be sorted and re-sorted for display and for other children to develop further. Paper was ordered cheaply, direct from a local paper merchant, or offcuts were purchased in bulk from a local printer. Colours similar to metals were selected – browns of all kinds and greys, white, black, cinnamon, buff, pale yellow, dull orange. Water colours with small brushes, bought in separate pans, were given as a special treat and were presented still in their wrappings so that the children could read the unfamiliar names of the colours:

burnt sienna	cadmium yellow	sepia
burnt umber	lemon yellow	raw umber
yellow ochre	gamboge	Vandyke brown
Indian red	Davy's gray	mineral blue
ivory black	charcoal grey	indigo
lamp black	Chinese white	steel.
blue black	oxide of chromium	

Pastels and oil pastels were provided in black, white, yellow ochre, burnt sienna, burnt umber, grey, gamboge, Payne's grey, Naples yellow, red orange, Sprink's citron, madder brown. Conté crayons were another treat in black, white, red sanguine, and sepia bistre. Cheaper working materials included a supply of charcoal, as well as blackboard chalks and Brusho inks in white, brown, and yellow. Wax crayons were ordered in suitable colours and children were encouraged to bring pencils, black biros, and fibre-tipped pens in black, brown, yellow, and grey. This selection made a great impact when the working materials were presented with the museum's loan collection of metal work. It helped the children to savour and to record the qualities of the material they were studying. The sensitivity and enthusiasm aroused by study at the museum was instrumental in helping the school to achieve such intensive preparation.

After the visits to the Worcestershire County Museum, the children decided they would have their own museum of metal work. It built up remarkably quickly and, because children in this school move informally from room to room to see each other's work, the interest spread until six classes were collecting, each in their own room. Although it is difficult to give any idea of the enormous range of material that was brought, this selected list may help:

miner's lamp	glass-working tongs	parachute hook
bottle mould	branding iron	brass weights
shoe last	horse bit	lock
wrought-iron scroll	horse shoe	copper preserving pan
badge dyes	sledge-hammer	jelly mould
type settings	clock parts	old thimble
mole trap	pocket balance	curling tongs
fox trap	trivet	

Reference books were provided and the children searched through them for information about their collection. They needed encouragement and training before they learnt to observe objects carefully and to have faith in their own findings. Once they realized how far they could go in their own right the work took on a vigorous and personal quality.

The flat iron is heavy. It weighs 5 pounds 7 ounces. It is the heaviest we have by 14 ounces, is 5 inches high and $6\frac{1}{2}$ inches long and 4 inches where it is widest. I don't think its ironing area is as big as our electric iron at home.

The iron has a number on it which is five and it is more rusty and knobbly on top than it is underneath where it is smooth and only a bit rusty. They were always rusty every time you used them my gran says and you had to press them and rub them backwards and forwards on some paper with some gritty powder on it and if you didn't I expect they would make your clothes rusty.

My mum says when she was little her mum used the flat iron what I brought to school and the only way what you knew the iron was hot enough to iron was you spit on it and if the spit made a sizzle and jumped off again it was hot enough but the handle was hot too. The kids made their mums iron holders so they did not burn their hands and they made them with bits of cloth or knitting.

Soon the collections became unmanageable and, after discussion, it seemed

Part of the collection of metal objects

Classification begins

sensible to group some items together to form specialist areas of metal objects
in a school museum. There were, for instance:

17 flat irons and charcoal irons
a range of equipment for weighing and measuring
a large number of craftsmen's tools
10 nineteenth-century metal money boxes in the form of animals and
    human figures with mechanical or semi-mechanical action
a variety of hand-made nails
a box full of old keys
eighteenth- and nineteenth-century hinges and latches
a large collection of cog wheels
samples of wrought iron.

Organization

A card index system was introduced at this point and every child who brought an object took a card, entering upon it the object, the donor, the place and date it was found, a description, and any information gleaned from books or local sources. The card was filed in the catalogue; then the child also made a label to go with his object in the museum.

The children were shown monographs from local museums and discussed their uses, what should go into them, what monographs the school should produce, and who should produce them. Thus they were introduced to some of the techniques of museum administration and the great conglomeration of metal objects was discussed, analysed, and sorted into groupings that gave a new impetus to observation and study in depth.

RANGE OF ACTIVITIES

Meanwhile investigations were constantly under way. Grandmothers, grandfathers, great uncles, and aunts all became interested, and various tales, original stories, photographs, and folklore were unearthed. Among these were the metal-workers' hymns, composed and spread in the Evangelical Revival and revived enthusiastically by the school children who would form groups in passages and playground to sing.

The children decided they wanted to take school prayers, using ideas and material developing from their metal-work studies and the headmaster promised to help them. 'We don't want help, Sir,' they replied, 'We want to do it ourselves.' And this they did, choosing their hymns, composing the prayers, selecting passages about metals from the Bible, and describing the appalling conditions under which the people had worked:

The children used to get up about five o'clock in the morning to go to school but they first helped their mums in the nail shop and some used to die before they were five years old because of terrible diseases. The children that went home for dinner had to take their fathers' dinner to them at work and the teachers were very strict and even if you held the pencil in the wrong hand you got shouted at. One man made 170,000 nails in a fortnight and he did not still get a lot of money for them. They worked hard and they were poor all the time in the darkness of the smoke.

For only Og, King of Bashan, remained of the remnant of giants; behold,

Children made a metal train after studying the transport of metals

his bedstead was a bedstead of iron – is it not in Rabbath of the children of Ammon? Nine cubits was the length thereof, and four cubits the breadth of it, after the cubit of a man.

This image's head was of fine gold, his breast and his arms of silver, his belly and his thighs of brass. His legs of iron, his feet part of iron and part of clay.

There was only one thing wrong with assembly that day. It took half the morning.

Historical and geographical information was incorporated, almost unconsciously, into the recording of details of objects. Mathematics played a large part because some unique measuring and weighing tools were unearthed and teachers took the opportunity to devise work cards, problems, comparisons, and practical work centred on these collections.

Several children decided to find out how many metals and alloys they could discover and to be informed on the appearance and properties of each. Scientific investigation proceeded with experiments and with magnets. Some of the magnets used with pins, shreds of metal, and iron filings made such beautiful patterns that it was decided to call in a lecturer from a college of education to discuss possibilities for creative work. This man, a sculptor

in metal, brought a group of boys to his college to watch students operating oxy-acetylene equipment. Back at school he helped children to construct a small furnace in which metal could be melted in a crucible. Then a large metal box tray was filled with casting sand. The children packed it tight and, pressing fingers into the surface, excavated simple shapes to fill with molten metal. There was great excitement as they waited for the aluminium, lead, or tin to cool so that they could dig out the little globules and nodules they had cast. They were also shown how to beat out blisters of repoussé pattern on sheet metal, how to curve it, or how to punch, prick, and pockmark the surface by hammering at it with nails and strips of metal filed in simple shapes. The strength of this work lay in its experimental approach and its entirely unpretentious quality. More sustained fantasies were created with small scrap metal of all kinds – cog wheels, clock parts, tiny springs, the insides of valves and electrical equipment, metal turnings, copper and galvanized wire, brass rings and rods, steel beads and buttons, every variety of tubing. These collections were then patiently assembled by means of adhesives into constructions of incredible complexity. Several girls also tried pattern-making in metals, pressing nuts and bolts, nails and screws, staples and rivets of all kinds into slabs of plasticine. The geometric forms of these patterns were obviously derived and developed from the metal sample boards they had seen at the Worcestershire County Museum.

47

Interest in the metal study alternately grew and diminished over the months. Other studies and activities ran parallel to it, but it was in the ascendancy. It is not to be supposed that it interested all the children during that time; some children tired of the subject or even rebelled against it. The headmaster says:

One day a group of children came to see me in my room and asked if they could give up their study of metals, 'Why?' 'Please, Sir, it's got so that it's making us feel HARD inside.' 'What do you want to do?' 'Can we do something about people?' 'Stories?' 'Stories from the Bible, Sir.' 'Or fables.' Various suggestions were made and discussed, until eventually we came to Malory's *Morte d'Arthur*. This actually led, in the end, to an even greater impetus to the metal study, because the legend of Arthur described his armour and his sword, Excalibur, and so the whole consideration of protection by armour and attack by weapons arose. Although the emphasis was on the romantic aspect of literature, the children were still absorbed in the study of metals and ready to pick it up given any opportunity.

VISITS

Throughout the months more visits took place. Sometimes two teachers went with a class, leaving in school children trained to be self-reliant with work that was well under way; sometimes a small group would go with one teacher or with a tutor and students from a college of education. Occasionally the education officer of a museum would organize activities after discussion with the school. Visits were made to see:

> smelting at the steelworks in the Black Country
> the silver collection at the Birmingham Art Gallery
> scientific instruments at the Science Museum, South Kensington
> the armour at Warwick Castle
> the first iron bridge in Shropshire
> cast and wrought iron in the old streets of Stourbridge
> backyards with nailers' workshops in Lye and district.

Finances had to be carefully organized. The local authority paid for some local visits and parents made contributions for others. No child who wanted to join his group was debarred from an expedition, for the school fund operates for those in difficulty. Of the visits listed above, it may be helpful to study the one to the Birmingham Art Gallery.

The children had seen the casting of anchors and the forging of great chains. They had collected ancient and battered pots, kettles, preserving pans and a wealth of vigorous and sturdy metal work. Had not the time come to introduce them to such top quality material as the exquisite collection of Restoration and Georgian silver at the Birmingham Art Gallery? The school got in touch with the gallery's education officer, and she suggested that their expert on silver should have a session with a small group of children. Both the school and the expert approached this session with some trepidation. The expert worked with scholars and students; she had never handled a number of children before, let alone primary-school children. The teachers were uncertain how the children would react. There was a teacher–child relationship that had developed an easy exchange of ideas and enthusiasms, of conversation and inquiry, but this was a highly specialized subject, taken with an expert who had no pretensions to pedagogy. It seemed only too likely that the children might be bored. How could they be expected to enjoy the pieces with any degree of aesthetic sensibility?

On a table in the museum's schoolroom a selection of silver was available for the children to inspect and handle. The expert told them what to look for and was surprised and pleased that they were often fascinated by other qualities of their own choosing. They asked questions and were impressed by answers more comprehensive and scholarly than would have been possible from their own teachers. In short, the expert and the children were delighted with each other. She found their naive enthusiasm fresh and touching, a good many of their questions astute, and much of their enjoyment at a more sensitive level than had seemed possible. In many ways, she thought, there was an easier instead of a more difficult human relationship than with more sophisticated, older students. The children were not only thrilled with the silver, but awed by the opportunity to handle it, draw it at close range, and discuss it with someone who could deal with the subject in depth. There is no doubt that even young children have a healthy regard for the expert and, given the right conditions, have some appreciation and individual response to works of art.

Back in the gallery, in the permanent collection of silver, the teacher came into her own as she observed the children looking at the pieces with new understanding and relish. She noticed what individuals chose, for the choices and the conversation were revealing. A teacher can learn a great deal about her children by observing their reaction, and can encourage perception by listening sympathetically to what they have to say.

I like the little silver sweet dish best because I can guess how they made it and I would put Smarties in it because they are round and the patterns on the dish are like little round lumps that are shiny. I think they would go with it especially if you could get silver Smarties.

The teacher can send the children off to collect patterned borders or engraved coats of arms, or to find the platter with the handsome, heavily worked beasts and birds, the peacock, camel, unicorn, and turkey. Which pieces have fan and shell forms and which are worked in ways that are reminiscent of the techniques in metal working which the children have used themselves in school?

CONCLUSION

There is nothing remarkable in these methods. They are in common use in many schools, with school museums and visits to museums either stimulating or intensifying interests. Written up in this way the sequence may sound dangerously like an over-controlled development. In practice, though, it 'proceeded with all the uncertainty that attends any creative activity' and the points that have been selected sprang from an altogether wider field of activity. The work became so vigorous, with a multiplicity of ideas – some stillborn, others flourishing but unrecorded here – that it continued to run for some time, spread throughout the school, and made its own environment of piles of old iron waiting to be sorted, huge paintings of blast furnaces covering half a classroom wall, batches of written work set aside to be selected for monographs, groups of scientific and mathematical material touching off problems to be solved.

The museums had, each in their own particular way, made their contribution to a complex and sustained range of work involving environment, personal interests, varied subject matter, and creative activities. Children had learnt to know and appreciate the difference between wrought and cast metal, between old and new, between iron and steel, tin and lead, copper, brass and bronze, and between the repoussé opulence of a Restoration porringer and the crisp and elegant ornament on a Lamerie cup. Some children were fascinated by a precision job for industry, others had a natural liking for the past and the patina of age. 'Don't you go polishing that up because it won't look old no more.'

Chapter six

Museum services

Museums often provide a wide range of services – publications, photographic departments, libraries, advice from experts, lectures, films, refreshment facilities, and social events. In addition, some of them provide more purely educational services such as an education staff, workrooms, individual study booths, material for handling, darkrooms, an advisory service, children's clubs, loan collections, travelling kits and exhibitions, supplies of slides, film and tape recordings, vacation schemes and temporary exhibitions.

THE LOAN COLLECTION

Loan collections provide material for educational use. They vary from high-quality exhibits circulated by the Victoria and Albert Museum for regional museums, colleges of art, and colleges of education to modest collections circulated by local museums. The Derbyshire and West Riding educational authorities provide large collections for use by schools and highly organized loan services are also provided by the National Museum of Wales at Cardiff, and by some regional museums.

There is no evidence so far that children are allowed to select loan materials for their own use in the classroom; enjoyment and motivation for study might be enhanced if they could. Teachers, however, certainly appreciate the opportunities that a loan service provides. They know that these exhibits can enrich work under way, enliven the school environment, or touch off new experiences and an increasing range of activities. The following comments by teachers and museum education officers illustrate awareness of this potential:

Museum material is for us not only of great aesthetic value. It is integrated into the life of the school and stimulates expression in a variety of ways – including creative writing, painting, claywork, and work with base materials.

Loans should be regarded as ancillary to, but not as a substitute for, a museum. They can create a museum type of environment in the classroom but at a lower level of vitality. However desirable they may be in enhancing the school environment, the loan services are only one of many ways in which it should be improved.

A loan collection can supplement and enrich the main collection by giving opportunities for handling and for intimate and prolonged study. Children can then go back to the quality material with greater zest and deeper understanding.

An extensive local study project was carried out by a master at a rural secondary school. Assisted by loans of specimens from the school service of the National Museum and by advice from the archaeological department he encouraged his pupils to search the hillsides around their homes (largely in their own time) for pre-historic flint objects, ancient pottery and any small object of interest, whether man-made or natural. These were preserved in the school for some time. Later many of them were presented to the local museum. The recording and identification of specimens in the loan collection and their comparison with original geological or archaeological specimens are an interesting aspect of this service.

There is pressure on museums to set up loan services. This is understandable and, if school attendance at museums continues to increase, it may be desirable to provide more alternative or intermediate services of this kind. At present, however, the smaller museums with loan collections and limited resources face problems of scarcity values and high prices, and there may therefore be a case for combined services covering a county or district which could then be more highly selective. The objectives of a loan service always need to be kept in mind. In some cases, museums appear to be spending a disproportionate amount of money on models of doubtful quality, when the needs of teachers might be more satisfactorily met by referring them to original material in the neighbourhood or to local buildings or exhibits in local collections. A collection of loan material should be developed in relation to the total teaching resources of the environment – resources that should be catalogued and made known to teachers through teachers' centres or the education departments of museums. The thoughtful way in which one museum loan service operates is described by a museum education officer as follows:

We try to indicate by the use of display techniques involving specimens the way in which children can begin to inquire into their environment. Since this environment is complex, we try to produce exhibits which, while specialising in one aspect, are also open-ended. An exhibit on exploring a building will thus contain techniques which children can apply to other forms of discovery and an exhibit on tracks and signs which shows marble galls, witch spoons, and animal tracks in sand, can be used to spark off interest which may well lead to research into the animal population of a sand dune area.

We are beginning to work closely with teachers' centres which act as distribution and collecting centres for the loan service, distributing loan cases to 14 schools. The South Molten Centre has asked for help in staging an exhibition on environmental studies in which the museum service will provide the central core; this will be surrounded by children's work. We anticipate that the central theme will travel from teachers' centre to centre.

We try to develop the curriculum through environmental studies in the field and very much time is spent with classes out of doors. Classes of children from infant to A level are taken by the officer to woodlands, estuary, moor and sea shore.

Working closely with the Nature Conservancy, nature trails have been established and the museum service role in this co-operative effort was to produce displays which are placed along the trail. Loan items on woodland ecology and sets of slides and photographs of the area are provided as starters or follow-up material.

An experiment using loan material

Loan material as a starting point, loan material for reference, for recording, for identification, related to the main collections, to the environment – these imaginative uses indicate the potential of the service. Loan material, for example, as earlier comments pointed out, can be used to stimulate valuable creative work in schools. A carved wooden pig from New Guinea, loaned by a museum to a college of education, became a focal point of experiment for the students, for children in a primary school being taught by the students, and for the graphic department in a school of art where the children's creative work was assembled in book form.

The six-year-old children were amused and delighted when the pig was introduced to them. The pattern, particularly, had to be studied carefully. Observation was surprisingly intense and exact. In a short time they found that the pattern on one side was not the same as on the other, they had to know why it stopped halfway down one leg, how it was put on the pig, why it was white. Questions came thick and fast and, as often as not, were returned for them to think out for themselves. They stroked his flanks, followed the grooved lines with finger tips. They were prepared to look for a long time.

We broke it up in the end and asked them to draw their favourite bit of pig pattern, an assignment which made them look harder still. They are used to drawing and writing on the same page so we got some writing too.

During subsequent visits the children became very fond of the pig but, as conversation about jungles, hunters and killings developed, a few of them became frightened. They looked askance at him and talked of him with bated breath. He even, at one stage, seemed to assume larger proportions and an almost mystical presence. One child said he was a bad pig. People, she said, should be frightened of him. She seemed to sense evil there. The split in his stomach fascinated some. This, they said, was where he had been killed. Much talk of knives, blood, bloody, bleedy, dead, deaded, bleedy-deaded. One student said he was reminded vividly of William Golding's *Lord of the Flies*. Other children were more tender hearted. They refused to let the pig go and stroked and cuddled him. They bandaged his stomach, took his temperature and administered pills. No, they said to the hunter group, no visitors.

One boy has a father who keeps a pig farm. There are only some things, he insists, about our pig that are like a real pig. Patiently he points out the differences. He wants to draw a real pig for us. Yes, he'll write about it too. And the pig farm. We fetch him a photograph of a real pig to show we understand.

A little girl, on the other hand, was absorbed in the carved pattern. She was the only child who copied the pig-pattern logically, observing the parallel lines moving together into scroll forms. When asked if she would like to make up her own scroll patterns she took the paper and pastels offered and, without comment, set to work. She continued steadily in her own time and at home and turned out batches of work. If she flagged a little all that was needed was new paper – different kinds, sizes, colours or proportions – or a change of media from pastels to felt-tipped pens or from pencil to watercolour. With new impetus she would set off again in an endless set of variations on scroll patterns with a fascinatingly personal use of colour.

Three pigs have
6 eyes
3 noses
3 tails
4 trotters
200 bristles

Conversation and make-believe gradually developed into stories. The children's stories exploited what they had been told and what they had discovered and felt. We had stories about the man who carved the pig, how the pig came to Birmingham, and how he lived in the forest. We had tales and poems about the Magic Pig, the Fairy Pig and the King of the Patterned Pigs. They responded to the quality of fantasy in the object with their own sense of fantasy. These are some of the comments they made as we talked:

> This is the best bit of pattern.
> I seen patterns like that on tombs.
> What's tombs?
> Them's what they puts over dead people when they bury them.
> And they put patterns on them like they put patterns on the pig.
> The pig should be buried because of his bad cut on his tummy.
> He is a dead pig.
> We could make him a tomb with his own pig pattern on it.
> Why did they have tombs?
> I haven't ever seen one.
> They don't give them to pigs. They only give them to people.
> They eat the pigs.

'The pig is taking them for a ride. The lady has a little boy. He may fall off.'

They couldn't eat this pig because he is wood.
My Mummy would like this pig. She would
   put it on the mantelpiece and
   he would look pretty there.
My mum would think he was soft like.
Your mum's daft.
I know she is.
He's a heavy pig. I can't keep holding him up.
Put him down because I want to stroke him.
He feels a nice pig. A fat pig.
A smooth pig.

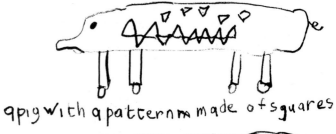

a pig with a pattern made of triangles

a pig with a pattern made of squares

Many art museums and museums of natural history provide children's clubs. They are usually held on a Saturday morning and in many cases a room is provided for creative activities such as painting and modelling.

Sketching in the galleries generally precedes or follows practical work. The clubs introduce children to the museum and help to make it a familiar and acceptable part of their everyday life. For some it becomes a place of personal enjoyment to which they return each week with pleasure. Their own work leads to discoveries in other galleries and should in turn lead to other museums and relate to outside interests both in the school and in the home. When this does not take place, there is need for a more imaginative approach. One such approach is reflected in the work of a Junior Discovery Club run by a regional museum, which occasionally uses its collections as 'starters' for activities outside the museum walls. The education officer says:

Since the club started, the range of activities has increased considerably to include related visits outside the museum, and linked sessions leading to the production of small plays using 'home-made' shadow puppets and masks. The only restriction placed on subjects dealt with is that activities are based on initial use of museum material, but this has, of course, always acted as a stimulus not a hindrance.

In future developments, we feel that more use could be made of the galleries because many children wander round the museum either before or after the Junior Discovery Club. Exercises using specimens on display could be thought out and this approach has already been tried with some success. The children were asked to choose an object on display and write a 'story' about it, either a factual account or an imaginary story. The stories submitted were of a high standard and covered a wide range of subjects.

A member writes about his club: In this club which is held at the museum every two weeks, you can learn a lot and have a lot of fun at the same time. At every meeting you do something new, unless, of course, you need more than one meeting for a particular topic. You also visit many places which you might not otherwise know about; for instance we have been to Ainsdale Nature Reserve where we learnt all about different types of flowers and trees; we have been on a car-ferry, where we were taken on the bridge and shown how the boat is controlled; and we have been to Pilkington's Glass Museum where we learnt all about the history of glass-making right up to the present day.

Some clubs also sponsor activities for children during the school holidays. These take many different forms – for example, specialist talks relating to

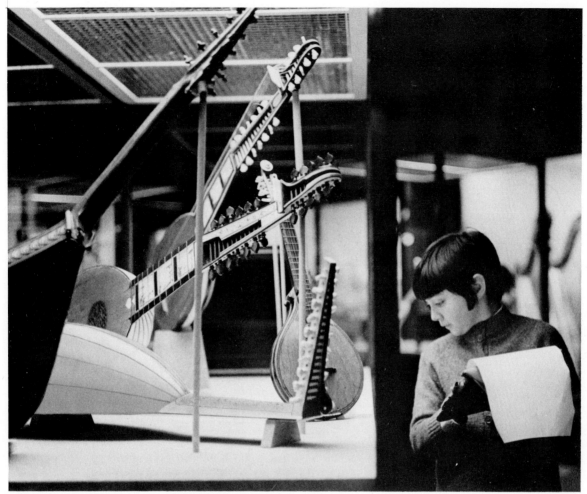

A member of the Saturday morning club at the Victoria and Albert Museum

children's exhibitions, or activities that include study in art galleries and opportunities for creative work. One group in a rural area made a house-to-house collection for bygones for a temporary exhibition relating to the neighbourhood. They were given space in the museum to set up their exhibition; they prepared labels and used reference books recommended by the staff, and expert help was to hand if required. In other cases, drama

57

enthusiasts use the museum as a reference library for costume and stage settings; enthusiastic photographers are encouraged to focus on an object of their choice, become interested and involved by means of their camera. Sometimes the museum directs interest to the environment, to the study of sites or buildings in the neighbourhood that relate to objects on view in the museum. Competitions that require observation, writing or sketching are popular.

It is surprising to find that science museums in this country so far play little part in sponsoring science clubs for children. Most club developments here take place in museums of art or natural history. But loan exhibitions to regional museums from the Science Museum in London could well be used to encourage the development of clubs and practical activities, although this is not envisaged in the museum's original aim. There is surprisingly little reference to the use of science museums in education other than specialist talks and guided tours. One of the few science studies relating to museums that was brought to our notice was carried out by a teacher at a middle school. He has produced a kit of materials on motor cars suggesting ways in which teachers can develop work on this topic by making use of the Motor Museum at Beaulieu. His kit is based on units developed by the Schools Council's Science 5–13 Project and copies are to be kept at the local teachers' centre for use by other teachers. An account is given in Appendix C.

TRAILS

A number of museums have established nature trails. A trail suggests an adventure, a series of discoveries, encounters with the unexpected. Children, one hopes, will be mentally on their toes, all senses alert. Overstructuring this experience, telling them what to see, where and when and how, takes away a great deal of the tension and the effort. The adventure trail becomes a tram line with the halts clearly defined. There may well be stopping-places as there are halts on a safari where game is likely, and the stopping-places may be geared for observation and stocked with specimens and information in the manner of a museum, but when the children set off on their trail, they must know that they have a sporting chance of spotting something which nobody has discovered before. It might be a strange slug, peculiar markings on a leaf, a root washed up by a stream, or an unidentifiable sound. At the end of the trail they should be able to check their personal discoveries with some of those that others have found before them. They must know of things they missed, why they missed them, and how they might learn to observe more keenly and deduce more accurately from their own first-hand observation.

These trails, following flora and fauna, geography and geology, sites and buildings, are mostly out of doors, though some lead through a museum. It would be an adventure, for example, to organize a trail to take children into the riches of the study collections, where they could discover birds and flowers on the porcelain, stitches familiar and unfamiliar on the embroideries, inlays and veneers as well as shapes and forms on furniture. In art galleries, they could explore the fauna and flora in landscapes, or in styles of buildings or ships, and so learn to see and appreciate a painting by Rubens or a seascape by Turner.

SPECIAL COURSES

A museum of art offers an introductory course on the history of art and design to sixth formers who still have a month at school after taking their A level examinations:

It is designed primarily for those intending to study the humanities at universities or colleges of art. It is held three days a week and includes illustrated lectures, filmshows, study sessions, and tutorials in the galleries. Full use is made of the collections for discussion and study and the staff contribute their skills and expertise.

There is enormous scope for the provision of other specialist services of this kind to stimulate the interest of older students. Too often the museum focuses its activities and services on the needs of the younger age groups and makes little attempt to overcome examination and syllabus difficulties and involve the fifth- or sixth-former.

PUBLICATIONS

Publications are an important part of the services offered by the museum to the public. Both national and regional museums show an increasing awareness of the public's interest in reproductions, slides, and booklets, etc. They now provide a wide range of visual and printed material, and in many museums the sales counter has been replaced by a vast display and sales area. Little attempt has so far been made, however, to find out if the needs of the school

59

and adult public are being satisfied. Is the choice of colour slides satisfactory? Are the non-specialist publications suitable for children? Which type of booklet do children prefer? Do they prefer cards or slides? Should special publications be prepared for different school age groups? These are only some of the questions to be asked. Teachers and museum education officers could profitably collaborate to provide some of the answers.

DISPLAY

Display presents problems both to the museum curator and to the forward-looking teacher. It is a matter of concern that museums are more and more organizing their material into teaching exhibits and, in the process, are thinning out the cases in order to put across a particular point of view more effectively. Thinning out a display does not, however, always make it more intelligible. Less organized display often presents more interesting opportunities for children to group for themselves and to find interesting relationships and cross references. To follow their own lines of inquiry, they require ample material to work with – serried rows of objects, cases filled with specimens of all kinds – shells and corals, crystals and fossils, folios of prints, rows of spoons. This description of the Pitt-Rivers Museum at Oxford shows what is wanted:

It is like a great tithe barn in which all kinds of wonderful objects from perhaps hundreds of pre-industrial societies have been brought and deposited. It is one of the most fascinating places I know. I have wandered about there many times and discovered things I never knew existed. Unlike most museums, in this crowded Victorian structure attached to the back of the Natural History Museum, you have the feeling that no man of taste has decided what is beautiful and what is not, or even what is important and what is not.

The arrangement of the museum allows you to appreciate this, because things are grouped not according to the culture that produced them but comparatively: similar objects or activities from cultures over the whole globe are put together. You see how incredibly elastic the form of any everyday object really is; you see how relative, even provincial, is our own orthodoxy of functionalism and convenience. For example, there is a section of combs. It ranges from the few heavy prongs of the Zulu comb to Chinese and Japanese combs which are like kinds of delicate filter. The section of clothes ranges from the brilliant Oceanic million-bird-feather cape to the grey-green Eskimo weathersuit made of the intestines of seals. (G. Brett, 'Travellers' Trophies')

60

Again in the matter of display, a well-known art historian and scholar has this to say:

Few people concerned with museums need to be told that what we want of them is self-effacement, that all their methods should be directed towards letting the object speak for itself without unnecessary distractions. Sometimes, however, I feel that display still underrates the power of concentration that belongs to the contemplative state of mind which the museum should foster. The great drive for selectivity, for spacing out the exhibits, may be due to this psychological mistake. Those who withdraw to the stillness of a museum may be much more capable of concentration than they are usually given credit for. The idea that an object can only be seen if it is surrounded by vast empty spaces is belied every day of our lives. We can read a news-paper column without even noticing the adjoining print; we can look at a picture book without being disturbed by the picture on the opposite page. A display case full of 18th century snuff boxes will not prevent a lover of these dainty objects from looking at them one by one. All we gain from radical 'thinning out' is the doubtful advantage of preventing the visitor from choosing for himself. Willy-nilly the director becomes the arbiter of taste, and styles not considered to be in tune with present trends are in danger of being forgotten altogether.

He goes on to suggest that

. . . the secondary or study collections should always be accessible without special application, to be explored not only by connoisseurs but even more eagerly by the curious in search of novel discoveries. It should be possible to encourage a frame of mind which finds the study collection especially attractive precisely because things are not there presented 'on a platter'. (E. H. Gombrich, 'Should a museum be active?')

These and other. problems that have been briefly touched on call for more consultation and closer co-operation between school and museum, between teacher and education officer. The initiative in establishing existing services has for the most part come from the museum. Now is the time for them to be supplemented by suggestions from teachers.

The following proposals have been put forward by a primary-school teacher about amenities that he thinks museums should provide:

I should like a correspondent to establish contact with the children before and after visits. An even more personal contact was made with a London museum when two members of the museum staff visited the school and saw the children's work, some of which was then displayed at the museum.

We need booklets, etc., to help in preparation. A plan of the museum is sometimes of particular interest – to be studied, copied, or enlarged by the children. Also a separate cloakroom for children for coats and sandwich bags, etc., which can be recovered at any time; plenty of seats in the galleries; some writing surfaces (some museums provide boards but young children find these difficult to handle) or counters or ledges round some exhibits; a double label – the detailed academic adult one and a simplified label aimed at, say, a nine-year-old child; a child's meal room with a soft drinks bar.

Most children like to buy postcards, pamphlets, etc., which help their work. It is rather disappointing at some museums to find only expensive guides and books at adult level.

And this comment comes from a member of a university institute of education:

The museum must develop its organisation for teaching. This surely means something more than providing a room into which children can be shepherded; it indicates a greater flexibility of arrangement, the possibility of different uses of galleries for as yet unexplored purposes; it may mean new methods of storage and encapsulation in order that relevant material may be readily assembled. If the educational use of museums is to develop as it should, this may mean that museums should become a new kind of institution.

Chapter seven

Relationships between schools and museums

It is clear that a more organic relationship must develop between the museums and the schools. If the education staff of the museum is to work closely with teachers – and this closeness should often be what we think of as team teaching – then a great deal of co-operative preparation will be called for. Besides this, the museum staff will need to become familiar with that part of the work which goes on in schools, and the teacher for his part will need to be more knowledgeable about the museum, its contents and its capabilities.

This is the view of one educationist. Another provocative view is this:

Let me say at once that I hate the idea of museums being used as teaching aids of any sort. Their first job is to house valuable objects safely and display them attractively. Where objects of high quality are concerned, our deepest response is to the object itself, not to an understanding of how it was made or used. A museum's main responsibility is not to broaden our minds but to make our scalps prickle in front of masterpieces and to create an environment which interferes with this experience as little as possible.

The second responsibility is to those who already are educated – to the student, the collector, the informed amateur. Objects are in museums because they are specially precious or rare, and their display and accessibility should be determined by the needs of those who know what they want to see. I will put comfortable study rooms, a constantly revised catalogue and a speedy photographic service above any expenditure for educating the casually inquisitive visitor or parties of school children. (John Hale, 'Museums and the teaching of history')

These statements are not as greatly opposed to one another as might appear at first sight. Indeed, it is part of an effective co-operation between museum education officers and teachers that each should have opportunities to learn to appreciate the other's problems and functions. Some museum education officers have a narrow conception of the nature of a school visit to a museum, perhaps because they have not experienced the pleasure and concentration with which a child can react to exhibits that interest and please him, provided he is given the opportunity. For their part, it is desirable that teachers should learn to appreciate exhibits in their own right and not merely as useful illustrations to their teaching. The use of objects to illustrate work under way is of course valid, but it is only one of the many ways of using museum resources. A genuine appreciation of a collection for its own sake will lead to new enjoyment and satisfaction and provide a basis for a good working relationship between teachers and museum staff.

There is undoubted need for better consultation between them. Teachers frequently complain of lack of information about local as well as national museums, while museum education officers may be in touch with schools who are regular visitors but have little or no opportunity for informal discussion with a wider range of teachers. They have few opportunities to keep abreast of curriculum developments or to suggest how museums can assist in carrying out new ideas. The recent dramatic growth in the number of teachers' centres should, however, provide more opportunities than have been available in the past for teachers and museum staff to discuss problems and new approaches.

Most museums publish leaflets, available on demand, with information about their various services and educational facilities. These often give useful guidance on questions such as size of groups, how to arrange a visit, and whom to contact. Too often, however, this information is available only at the museum and it is taken for granted that teachers know about these services, that they are ready to use them, and are willing to make the initial approach. Another difficulty is that if an information sheet is sent to the headmaster, it does not follow that it will be seen by other members of staff. The time factor is all-important and it is often lack of time as well as lack of opportunity that hinders the initial contact.

TEACHERS' CENTRES

Teachers' centres could play an important part in promoting museum education. Here teachers and museum staff could meet to discuss opportunities and developments; they might also view exhibitions of museum material and of children's museum work. Such facilities could be a great help to teachers entering new districts in getting to know the material in the new environment. A centre could collect and correlate information and stock equipment, perhaps in the following categories:

(a) Information on local museums and their collections, staffing, working facilities, publications, etc.

(b) Private collections and local school collections, together with other local opportunities for observing and collecting (e.g. a range of old medicinal objects in a chemist's shop, shells and corals in a pet shop, a good junk stall in a market, a sculptor's studio, a farm kitchen and dairy, a botanical garden).

(c) Links between museum objects and material in the environment (e.g. all of the tin mining and clay pit material in the Truro Museum that illustrates Cornish industries).

(d) Links between museum objects and material in the local record office.

(e) A list of local experts willing to give talks in schools or to help take school parties round museums to supplement school staff.

(f) A collection of books on museum education.

(g) Records of work already done in local museums.

(h) A fund of photographs, film, slides, tapes, and duplicated sheets on museum education.

(i) A map of the district plotting points of local interest.

(j) Cameras for children and teachers to use for recording in museums, a dark room for processing.

(k) A photocopier of good quality to duplicate children's drawing and writing, photographs, information, work-sheets, questionnaires, etc.

EDUCATION DEPARTMENTS OF MUSEUMS

Changes are taking place, however, and there is evidence that education departments in museums are trying to improve their publicity and widen their contact with schools. This note of change is reflected in the following account of a co-operative venture by one museum and a local primary school.

The headmaster was anxious to introduce the museum as an added resource to his staff. It so happened that one of his teachers was contemplating a project on trees and since she was not scientifically inclined it was arranged that the museum education officer would deal with the scientific/mathematical aspects, e.g. species growth, economic importance, commercial use, pests, etc. This involved the officer in one day's work a week at the school and to all intents and purposes on that day he was a member of the staff. The whole programme was carefully co-ordinated and included several visits.

The museum as a stimulus for related activities.
Children made their costumes and acted out Beowulf.

There is no doubt in either the headmaster's or the officer's mind that this was of value to both sides. It introduced not only the individual teacher but other members of staff to a new source of material and many new ideas. This was reflected in increased use of the museum's loan service and a better appreciation of the museum's potential. It also provided regular teaching experience for the museum staff and gave them a chance to keep abreast of current educational practice.

This type of co-operation gives new insights to both school and museum. The same museum has been experimenting with week-end courses for teachers and has established a close relationship with schools by setting up an advisory panel consisting of seven teacher representatives, one advisory teacher from each LEA in the area, one representative of each college of education, and three co-opted members appointed by the museum. The museum education officer acts as chairman. Members serve for three years and can be re-elected.

Another museum education officer has this to say about links with schools:

I regard links with teachers as of two types: those where there is regular contact and those where contact is occasional. The regular links consist of:

Newsletter – published each term and sent to all county schools: information about museum developments, descriptions of galleries, loan service additions, occasional articles on particular studies by schools or colleges.

Advisory Panel – meets each term and consists of teachers of all levels, i.e. heads, deputy heads, ordinary teachers, representing all types of institutions, colleges of education, secondary, junior and middle schools. The work of the museum education service is discussed and suggestions are made on content of loan material. A sub-group has been formed to prepare a history of the county for school use.

Teachers' Centres – recently established in the county – groups have attended the museum and are likely to form local committees concerned with education in museums, its possibilities and methods of work. Exhibitions of museum material to be mounted in these centres from time to time.

Museum Store – Loan Material – to be opened regularly outside school hours to enable teachers to examine loan material and discuss with museum's education officer new loan material.

Museum Sub-Committee – has teachers' representative – this enables teachers to take part in the overall running of the museum.

The occasional links include:

Courses – held periodically for teachers from different types of schools; intended to show possibilities open to schools at the museum.

Inspectorate – both local and national have visited and receive information about the museum.

Visits – an attempt is made to meet and talk to all teachers bringing parties to the museum both at the start and finish of their visit.

This museum's officer stresses that he does not direct the work done by teachers. He may make suggestions to them but no pressure is put on them to follow any particular line or method. He conceives his role as that of a liaison officer between the museum staff, the collections, and the school. He is not a director.

COLLEGES OF EDUCATION

A similar approach was adopted by a college of education in a week-end course for teachers. The course was designed 'to give opportunities to enjoy museum exhibits; for individuals to develop personal response through writing, art, drama, discussion, historical, and geographical discovery, integrated studies or any other activity of their own choice.' There were lectures, visits to local museums, and discussion with teachers and visitors from a wide educational background. Exhibitions showed work developed from museum material, ranging from activities in an infant school to studies in a college of education. The practical activities, lectures, and discussions were all related to progressive teaching situations and the museum itself was considered as part of the educational environment.

But how far are colleges of education preparing their *students* to make effective use of museum resources? One lecturer says:

We can train teachers for museum work if we want to do it. We can put on museum courses as we put on courses for backward readers, for environmental studies, for practical mathematics. It is a matter of priorities. It may be that a museum course should be one of a wide range of options put on by colleges of education so that students with natural interests and enthusiasm for the work would be able to choose this opportunity to learn to use museums well.

The optional course on museum studies planned by one college is described as follows:

This course will explore work with children in national and local museums. It will also cover school collecting and permanent school museums. Activities will cut across disciplines and involve studies of music, magic, children's toys, shells, fossils, sculpture, portraits, ships, agriculture, sociology, scientific instruments, industrial archaeology, religion, etc. It will relate museum material to the environment and show how environmental studies can be taken deeper in a more intense examination of study collections. A student taking this course should be able, not only to use museums with some purpose, but should be better equipped to tackle other integrated studies involving straightforward recording and creative work.

Many students from colleges of education do visit museums as part of their personal studies. This is to be encouraged, but the colleges should make students appreciate that children can be given similar opportunities for study and pleasure; opportunities should also be provided for the student to work with children in museums in the course of their teacher training.

OPPORTUNITIES FOR TRAINING IN MUSEUM WORK

There is no doubt that teachers do not always understand the difficulties that beset museums. Even in large cities museums are understaffed and unable to meet demands made on them. Problems of control and organization vary according to schools' methods of work; the museum education officer can lack experience when dealing with over-excited, apathetic, over-demanding, or under-stretched children. Nevertheless, there appears to be more concern on the part of both museum and college to train the teacher than for the museum education officer to be given opportunities to come to terms with educational reforms in the course of his museum training or to have experience of forward-looking methods that encourage children to choose, to think, to feel, to record, and to learn. Courses on museology that include all aspects of museum work are now offered at universities in many countries. In this country a one-year course is given for post-graduates at the University of Leicester, and there is also a Museum Diploma Course organized by the Education Committee of the Museums Association. Students at each of these courses are given an overall picture of the requirements of the school-age public and in the course of their practical work in museums they have opportunities to study educational methods. Generally speaking, however, education does not figure largely in the year's programme. A working party on training, set up by the International Council of Museums, has recently made recommendations to the organizer of these courses concerning the qualifications, training facilities, and status of museum education officers.

Its report is worth quoting at length:

1. New attitudes in education are steadily replacing the formal, conceptual approach to learning which has dominated so much teaching in the past. Today there is an increasing awareness of the need to encourage methods of individual inquiry and the study of original source material. The teaching structure is becoming a joint venture in learning between child and teacher, and similar changes are taking place in adult education.

2. Education in the museum reflects this change in attitude. Until recently, it fulfilled a passive role; today, due in part to pressures and demands made by an ever increasing number of visitors, the whole concept of education in the museum is changing. Former traditional methods of talks, lectures and display no longer suffice. Its role has become more complex and includes problems of administration as well as modern techniques of communication. To meet these new requirements and to carry out an effective cultural and educational programme, the Working Party recommends: that a department of education be set up within the existing structure of the museum in charge of a curator, keeper or educator, according to the terminology used.

3. The work of this department is as specialised as that of other departments in the museum. Its first concern is to establish close and satisfactory communication between the public and the exhibits within and out of the museum (loan services, temporary exhibitions, clubs, etc.). To this end, the curator or educator must be trained to identify the different categories of visitors, understand their motives in coming to the museum and satisfy their needs.

4. He must co-operate with other cultural and educational bodies of school age and be able to initiate the use of documentary and audio-visual media relating to the objects. To carry out this work effectively, the department should have premises specially equipped and a staff trained to achieve these objectives.

5. The Working Party accordingly recommends that the training of the educationalist in the museum should include the following subjects:

    1. Techniques of communication (to achieve contact with the object by verbal, visual, practical media).
    2. Evaluation of the different categories of the museum public (the casual visitor, the specialist visitor, the scholastic public, etc.).
    3. Knowledge of up-to-date teaching methods and modern developments in education in relation to the museums.
    4. Certain aspects of museology, in particular problems of display in permanent collections, in temporary and circulation exhibitions and in loan services.
    5. Administration including financial matters.
    6. The administrative structure of education and cultural institutions with which he will co-operate.
    7. Activities within and without the museum (clubs, field studies, etc.).

8. The preparation of educational material for specific use with different categories of the public.

Suitable training for students, teachers, and museum staff is basic to the development of educational activities in museums. Interesting pilot work has been done by individuals but it is now a matter of urgency that institutions should co-ordinate their interests and plan together.

Chapter eight

Overseas developments

Growing interest in museums and concern for their use by the school and adult community is by no means limited to this country. There is evidence of this in the world-wide membership of the International Council of Museums (ICOM) which, by means of its international committees, has become a focal point for the exchange of information and ideas. These committees cover all aspects of museum activity, specialist as well as general, i.e. science and technology, natural history, international art exhibitions, applied art museums, conservation, regional museums, architecture and museum techniques, education and cultural action, musical instruments, museums of transport, etc. Conferences and seminars are held and experts sent on missions. It has a documentation centre at its headquarters in Paris, and is responsible for a quarterly magazine, *ICOM News*. It has also sponsored publications, several of which are concerned with education: *Training of Museum Personnel*, *Museums and Adult Education*, and *The Role of the Museum in Education and Cultural Action*, the report of a meeting held in Leningrad and Moscow in 1968, under the auspices of the National Committee of the USSR (see also Bibliography).

The International Council of Museums Committee for Education and Cultural Action has been active both in collecting information and in helping to instigate activities and research projects. Of particular interest is *The Museums' Annual*, a publication which has just started and whose purpose is 'to inform specialists in museums and in education of current events – programmes, projects, experiments, new techniques, training facilities, and surveys relating to the public.' It is also intended to act as 'a link between the national working parties on education and the international committee with a view to exchanging ideas and inciting activities, and . . . [to be] accepted as such by the authorities, teachers and others concerned with culture.' (*Museums' Annual*, No. 1, 1969.) Membership of ICOM is not restricted to museum personnel; it is open to all educationists.

Some of the most striking developments have taken place in countries faced with widespread problems of illiteracy and general education where the museum has been called on to play an imaginative and constructive role. In the USSR and in Poland, for example, museum visits by schoolchildren are an accepted and integrated part of the curriculum, and there is active co-operation between museums and adult recreation centres in the form of travelling exhibitions, lectures, discussion groups, etc. These activities also extend to industrial centres where talks are given during the lunch-breaks. The policy is obviously successful and museums are crowded.

The museum habit is strengthened by clubs for schoolchildren and for young adolescents. The Pushkin Museum in Moscow, for example, uses imaginative methods in study circles which children attend from pre-school up to their final classes:

The youngest draw. On Sundays you can see them – less than four years old – comfortably installed on the carpet or in front of an easel, drawing away happily. Others have various picture games with their monitors. Favourites are 'What does the picture contain?', and 'What is the pose of the statue?' After all have taken a careful look at the picture, one turns his back on it and the others question him about it. This simple game helps to enhance visual memory, concentration, and taste as well as knowledge. The statue game is even better. One child has to imitate the pose of the statue in front of him and the others must rectify anything wrong, all learning in the process how to see and represent the human body correctly. These lesson-games usually take place half an hour before the drawing lesson and induce an emotional frame of mind in which children draw whatever has struck their imagination. They are often told stories and legends of Egypt and Greece, tangibly backed by the actual works of art. From 9 to 14 the work becomes more serious, with drawings, sketches, compositions, still-lifes. (E. Larionova, 'The aesthetic education of children in the museum')

SCIENCE MUSEUMS IN INDIA AND EGYPT

India and Egypt, also concerned with problems of general education, stand out because of the special use they are making of science museums. For the most part these are of recent date and unhampered by tradition. The Birla Industrial and Technological Museum in Calcutta provides training courses for teachers, travelling exhibitions, and science demonstration lectures both at the museum and at 'Creative Ability Centres'. The Science Museum in

Cairo has a highly organized programme, both for teachers and children. Emphasis is placed on direct contact and work with children, and an experimental centre has been set up in the museum for those who are 'gifted'. These are children who after a period of working in the museum are selected on account of their aptitude for science studies. They receive special training from the museum staff and have the use of museum laboratories and opportunities to take part in field surveys in the desert under the museum's supervision. Similar centres are being encouraged elsewhere in Egypt, and science clubs financed by the Ministry and by industrial associations are rapidly spreading. Children are being encouraged to buy inexpensive science kits with notes provided by the museum in order to carry out certain simple experiments. More elaborate kits are loaned by the museum to schools.

AN AMERICAN CONFERENCE

It is appropriate here to mention a conference on 'Opportunities for Extending Museum Contributions to Pre-College Science Education', which was held in Washington DC, in January 1970 and supported by the National Science Foundation. A report recently issued by the Smithsonian Institution summarizes the papers and discussions. These touched such diverse aspects of science teaching as: 'In the museum classroom', 'In the laboratory', 'On museum-conducted field trips', 'Education for future science studies', 'Teaching science in the inner city'. Related topics on wider education issues were also discussed such as 'Relationship between the centres and their communities' and 'Appraising effectiveness of open-educational experiments'.

The following extract from a paper by Emily Richards, 'The museum as a regional science curriculum research centre', puts forward some interesting suggestions:

A truly valuable regional science center would contain comprehensive collections of science curriculum materials: books, worksheets, equipment, films, and other teaching materials. The center would provide an informal setting for the hands-on investigation of curriculum materials. Individuals and groups of teachers and children could use the center to search for supplementary materials, to examine and consider alternative programs for adoption, or to construct programs from the available resources to meet the needs of their own schools. I picture something far more extensive than tables interspersed between shelves of books and packaged materials. I suggest generous amounts of open space which can be structured according to demands and which can house a wide range of types of curricular materials. Among these materials would be sandboxes, water tables, inclined planes, pendulums, balance boards, and plants and animals which can be easily maintained in the classroom. There would be facilities for review of audio-visual materials and for experimentation in the design of multi-media programs. There would also be a shop where teachers and children could build equipment for their classrooms. In addition, provision might be made for the display of architectural blueprints and mock-ups of innovative classrooms and science teaching materials.

OTHER DEVELOPING COUNTRIES

In other developing countries where science centres are not yet established, it is the art museum that is contributing to the education of the public. This is in line with early developments in museum education in the West where art museums have often taken the initiative. In Indonesia, the art and craft tradition is closely linked to the background of the people, and it is in the museum that this is being practised and encouraged. One might indeed say that there is here tangible evidence of education through art; dance, drama, and music are all-important. The museum is the centre of regular performances of the famed Wayang purna, the shadow puppet, and also of dance and of Indonesian music.

In countries in tropical Africa, efforts are currently being made to develop museum education services, even though the museums themselves are far from well-equipped. Funds, technical resources, and personnel are scanty by European standards, and climate and geography pose considerable obstacles.

A remarkable amount of new museum building has taken place during the last decade, as former colonial territories have achieved political independence. National museums have been established at Kampala (Uganda), Dar-es-Salaam (Tanzania), Lagos (Nigeria), and Accra (Ghana). At Nairobi the old Coryndon Museum has become the National Museum of Kenya.

These museums are aware of their potential role in education and all have instituted some form of educational service, usually with specially trained staff. They have concentrated in the first instance on establishing facilities for teaching and guiding parties of children and adults within the museum premises. Loan collections and travelling exhibitions are, as yet, in their infancy.

The immediate opportunities arise from the rich ethnographical and archaeological collections, interests inherited from colonial days. These

75

can help to make both teachers and pupils aware of indigenous traditions of art, craft, and culture, now in danger of being obliterated by Western influences; they can also show the significance of archaeology in revealing – for the first time – the antiquity of human cultural history in those countries. The education officers face challenging problems in seeking to relate the traditional values in art and craft to the contemporary, while the schools have exceptional opportunities to advance archaeological knowledge by their own discoveries.

SWEDEN

Interesting developments have taken place in Sweden over the past few years:

A decree by the King in Council of March 26, 1965 empowered the head of the Ministry of Education to call a number of experts to carry out a survey of museums, travelling exhibitions and other matters. The committee of inquiry which was duly set up came to be known as MUS 65.

MUS 65 turned out to be a rather unusual committee of inquiry in that its business included not only fact-finding but also practical experiments with actual exhibitions. The Riksutställningar, the National Scheme for Travelling Exhibitions, was part and parcel of a greater task allotted to MUS 65 covering among other things all aspects of museum activity in Sweden. To begin with, the experts were given the job of building up a brand new enterprise and providing a basic plan for the activities and policies to be pursued. A secretariat was set up in the autumn of 1965; at this stage it consisted of two persons. On this slender basis a full-scale experimental programme of exhibitions was developed.

Since that time the original secretariat of two has become a cultural institution with a full-time staff of over fifty people covering large areas of the country. During the year 1969/70 about 3·8 M Kroner were allocated to this experimental programme, and at present some 160 different exhibitions are on show, many of which have been produced in several versions. The objectives of the Riksutställningar are briefly to assess if exhibitions can be used to involve and activate people from all sectors of society, to discover what Riksutställningar can do to assist teaching and popular education and what service it should provide for museums.

Jointly with ICOM, the Riksutställningar has also prepared some experimental material for the educational training of museum personnel. The

ICOM documentary centre in Paris has prepared a folio of practical information on all known types of museum loan services. The Riksutställningar has prepared a 'kit on kits', a practical demonstration on preparing an exhibition. This includes panels with an assortment of bolts, screws, clips, and other technical gadgets; sets of coloured slides, 8 mm film, tapes, drawings, and photographs. A film, *The Museum as a Teaching Aid or How to Visit a Museum*, is part of this experimental training programme. Material in the film shows the work of many Swedish museums: Varberg, where children work with Stone Age tools, Gothenburg's museums of history and natural history, the Stockholm City Museum, and the Museum of Modern Art, where Carlo Derkert, Sweden's foremost 'animateur', is seen with a group of children who express their ideas in dance.

NEIGHBOURHOOD MUSEUMS AND CHILDREN'S CLUBS

Museum activities outside the museum proper are found both in Eastern and Western countries. Of special interest are the neighbourhood museums in the USA and children's clubs or creative centres such as Muse, the Brooklyn Museum, New York, and the Bal Bhavan, New Delhi.

The neighbourhood museum is becoming increasingly popular in the USA. It has something in common with the community centres elsewhere, but it relates more directly to the museum. Its aim is not only to bring the museum to people who for economic and social reasons rarely leave their neighbourhood, but also to identify them closely in its preparation, display, and in the activities that take place there. The exhibits often relate to the particular district. An account of the setting up of the Neighbourhood Museum in Anacosta, Washington DC, has been given in Chapter 2. These neighbourhood museums emphasize a basic consideration, that 'a central museum cannot pack up and move around the inner city, suburbs, or rural areas to meet the needs and requirements of any one community.'

Children's clubs, organized by the museum and held on museum premises, are increasing rapidly. They are developing far beyond the usual few hours spent there on a Saturday morning to become elaborate centres such as Muse (see Chapter 2), or the National Children's Museum at Bal Bhavan, New Delhi. The latter can be described as a creative centre. It has well-equipped workshops covering a wide selection of the arts and sciences: painting, drawing, collage, Batik, dance drama, and music as well as radio, electricity, star gazing, plants, and animal clubs. Situated in spacious grounds on the outskirts of a very poor neighbourhood from which it draws many of its members, it is so popular that, in order to take the maximum number, members are limited to a few hours' attendance per week. A children's museum is also in the grounds but is more frequented by visiting school parties than by casual young visitors. From an educational point of view, this venture is forward-looking and relates to the new learning situations being tried out in the West, where children are encouraged to create, to work, and to think as individuals.

By way of contrast here is a description of a club in the Boston Museum of Science, USA:

This Museum runs organized programmes for young people at three levels, of which the first is for children of from 4 to 9 years of age under the title 'Science Adventure Hour'. This is limited to 150 children, registered in advance, and accompanied to each session by an adult. The idea is to reach out to those children who have a special awareness of and curiosity about their environment, and to introduce them to the broad world of science through adventure in natural history, astronomy, and simple mechanics. The museum is convinced on past experience that, even at this tender age, eager fertile minds are seeking answers to their 'what?' and 'why?' questions about their environment. The Science Adventure Hour seeks to answer some of these questions and stimulate a deeper desire to know more.

The second level is called the 'Science Explorers' Programme' and deals with the age group from 10 to 16. Pupils must have been recommended for it by their teachers, and the course will use new teaching tools, demonstrations, lectures covering a wide sweep of science subjects, and experiments. Some of the lectures will be given by outside specialists as well as by the museum staff. The aim is to provide constant stimulation, motivation and intellectual excitement, and create vital awareness. Once fired, the young people will be encouraged to investigate by themselves in the library, with their teachers, or by personal consultation with the museum staff. The third level, called 'Science Frontiers' seeks to take advantage of the unusually high concentration of world-renowned scientists in the New England area, by having them present their discoveries, and discuss them, with the best young scientific minds of the area. Again, the participating young people of high-school age must have been selected by their teachers because of their superior talent, and the programme is designed to be a two-way affair. The young people are put in contact with the best professional scientists; the scientists are exposed to the searching questions of the best young science students – and only those who have tried this sort of session can really know just how searching these questions can be. (R. A. Stevens, *Out of School Science Activities for Young People*)

This cross-section of educational activities in museums reflects national policies and attitudes; these vary from the full integration of the museum in the school and post-school education, to individual developments, some of which receive official blessing and financial assistance. In most cases these developments are the work of enterprising initiative on the part of educationists in museums or those working in close association with them. The lavish expenditure of the Swedish Government in producing and trying out experimental material on a national scale is a new departure in the West, and may have unexpected repercussions in other countries.

Conclusion

In this report attempts have been made to assemble views and factual findings in all branches of museum education and to assess these in relation to the developing needs and requirements of schoolchildren.

There is strong evidence of the increasing use of museums by schools, and the following question must be asked: are museums sufficiently alerted and prepared for what could easily become an explosive demand from this potential public? Combined action is called for by schools and museums to prepare for this. It is not so much changes in the structure of the museum or demands for greatly increased staff that should be envisaged, but rather a more imaginative use of existing facilities and services; to ensure that the director and his staff are aware of the educational potential of their complex of galleries, study collections, and libraries; to consider how these should be linked to areas for group discussion, practical work, talks, loan collections, publication stalls, snack bar, or restaurant. It is a matter of appreciating new educational priorities so as to ensure greater flexibility in the use of the museum, for this is indeed the 'perfect open-ended learning situation' and should be regarded as the 'ideal library, laboratory or art centre'.

Tribute has been paid to such developments as school museums, to the amateur who helps to prepare, collect, and set up new museums. There is also scope for regional museums to establish local branches which might collaborate with teachers' centres in studies of the environment.

A phase of museum education is passing and in future we can hope to see less concentration on mere numbers of children visiting museums and more attention paid to working to greater purpose in a more sustained way. For teachers and museum staff this means greater effort, considerable preparation, and thought. They must ensure that new techniques and new equipment are used in the direct service of the children. It is also desirable in this co-operative planning that teachers should have personal experience of museum objects, that they themselves should have experienced the sense of pleasure and discovery that means so much to children, and that they too have opportunities to form their own impressions.

Above all, it is necessary to look beyond the established and preconceived setting to the freedoms foreshadowed by one of London's leading museum directors:

It is rare for museums ever to allow a spontaneous grouping of unconnected objects which belong together merely because they look beautiful and create a happy atmosphere, in which the ordinary visitor's mind is stimulated by unexpected confrontations – an El Greco next to a Van Gogh, an Elizabethan chest near an antique Persian rug. It gives the visitor an immediate sense of relaxation and beauty – information comes second, he does not feel that his mind is being brainwashed on the subject of Toulouse Lautrec lithographs or variations in 500 Greek pots. (Roy Strong, 'Martinis with the Bellinis')

It is this happy atmosphere, this sense of pleasure and delight that we would like to see associated with museums. We shall be pleased if our report makes a contribution towards this end.

Selected bibliography

Museums and Galleries in Great Britain and Ireland (Index Publishers, Dunstable)
Published annually. Lists collections in alphabetical order, giving times and cost of admission, and an indication of contents. It is an excellent guide for those who wish to know what material is available for study.

Historic Houses, Castles and Gardens in Great Britain and Ireland (Index Publishers, Dunstable)
Published annually. A comprehensive guide to houses, castles, and gardens that are open to the public, listed alphabetically by county. It includes a brief description of objects of historic interest in these collections, i.e. armour and books, tapestry and furniture, embroideries and inventories.

Museums Journal published quarterly by the Museums Association, 87 Charlotte Street, London W1P 2BX
Recent publications have included many articles on education and book reviews on the same subject.

Museum a quarterly review published by UNESCO, Place de Fontenoy, Paris 7
This publication covers all aspects of museum work. Volume XXI, No. 1, 1968, is concerned with the philosophy of museum education as seen by specialists working in museums and in education in Europe and in the USA.

The Museums' Annual/Les Annales des Musées published by ICOM (International Council of Museums), Unesco House, 1 Rue Miollis, Paris 15
The aim of the annual is to inform specialists in museums and in education in member countries (Europe, the Americas, the Near and Far East) of current events – projects, experiments, new techniques, training facilities, etc. – and to act as a link between national working parties set up by the International Committee of ICOM. No. 1, 1969, includes a bibliography of articles and publications on education listed by countries for the years 1967–69. No. 2, 1970, includes short articles, results of inquiries, news, and points of view, as well as reports of working parties and a selected bibliography.

Proceedings of the First International Conference on Education and Museums sponsored by the Committee for Education and Cultural Action of ICOM, held in Leningrad and Moscow, May 1968 (ICOM, 1969) Available from ICOM, Unesco House, 1 Rue Miollis, Paris 15 Includes contributions from Holland, India, France, Belgium, Poland, Czechoslovakia, USSR, USA and the UK.

The Museum: its History and its Tasks in Education by Alma S. Wittlin (Routledge & Kegan Paul, 1949) One of the first books dealing comprehensively with the subject which has become a classic in museum education.

Museums and Education by Eric Larrabee (Smithsonian Institution Press, Washington DC, 1968) Papers prepared for a conference at the University of Vermont which discuss the role museums should play in reinforcing and augmenting formal education. In this volume museum personnel, educators, government administrators, foundation representatives and others consider this vital question. Includes a useful bibliography.

Museums and Adult Education by Hans L. Zetterberg (Evelyn, Adams & Mackay, 1969) Museum services analysed by a sociologist with reference to different categories of visitors.

The Sacred Grove: Essays on Museums by Dillon Ripley (Simon & Schuster, New York, 1969; Gollancz, 1970) How museums have evolved from the 'cabinets of curiosities' of rich men, to play an increasingly important role within the community and to become centres of lively education.

Changing Museums by Molly Harrison (Longmans, 1967) Different aspects of museums as they relate to children – what the museum can offer, its role in visual education, how to plan a group visit, its contribution to the backward and handicapped. The bibliography includes a list of useful addresses.

The Listening Eye: Teaching in an Art Museum by Renée Marcousé (HMSO, 1961) Methods of approach that are primarily aesthetic are put forward in order to show how more effective use can be made of the art museum in education.

Children and Museums by Barbara Winstanley (Blackwell, 1966)

    Special reference to organized visits and loan services; how to make best use of museums when there are no school services, and suggestions on how to link museum visits with extra-mural activities; a useful bibliography.

Visiting Museums by Ann White (Faber & Faber, 1968)

    Lively suggestions on visits to eighteen museums, ten in London, eight in the rest of England, Scotland, and Wales. 'Come often; don't try to see too much at once', is the author's advice.

Museums in Education (HMSO, 1971)

    This survey (DES Education Survey No. 12) describes the range and variety of educational activity provided by those selected museums with which it was concerned. The implications of educational expansion are considered and the scope for future development is discussed.

Appendix A   Avoncroft Museum of Buildings: work cards

Work cards were designed for a particular group of junior children. They were available in the classroom during the study. Many were planned so that the children could solve the problems by observation, and were taken to the museum on subsequent visits. A wide choice of problems and questions ensured that each child would find something of interest. Children enjoy tackling open-ended work cards and relish difficult problems if they have been trained to think and encouraged to be adventuresome and self-reliant. A selection from the work card material is given below.

Discover different ways wood is fastened together.

If you could spend a day in the house with six friends, what would you do?

Make up a quiz for other children who visit Avoncroft Museum.

Why did they split the wood instead of sawing it?
Do you like the look of it done like this?

Pretend that you could cook a meal for olden times on the fire.
What would it be like?

What percentage of new wood do you estimate is used in the house?

Draw ideas for a school climbing frame to be constructed from timbers of demolished framework buildings.
How would exercise on this frame help you to appreciate construction?

Make rubbings of any interesting surfaces in the house.
Label the work and describe the surfaces you have chosen.

They used to char big logs slightly in the clearings in the forest so that they didn't smoke too badly when they were placed on the fire.
Paint a picture or make a clay model of people doing this.

If you could help to build the next house, what job would you choose?

Tell us about any house you would like to bring to the Avoncroft Museum. Draw and describe how it would look on the museum site when you had finished the job.

Choose any wall of the house. With illustrations, describe how it is constructed.

Calculate the number of tiles on the roof.
They are handmade. How can you tell? Draw one and describe it.
How are the tiles fixed to the roof?

Draw a plan of the house showing the strong room.
What was it used for and why was it put in this position?

You have been invited to a medieval party at the house.
How would you dress up for it?
You may, if you would like, make a fabric picture of your ideas.

How many square feet of light are admitted to the house by the windows?
How does this compare
  (a) with school
  (b) with your own home?
This is a difficult question. Do it with three friends who are good at mathematics and see how much you can tackle without any help.

Draw and write about an oak tree.
Try to do it by studying a tree, not by looking it up in a book.

Now look up a reference book and add other information.
Have you discovered anything the book left out?

Why are some timbers curved?

Do a picture of the fire as it would have been with the cooking pots and the big hunting dogs warming themselves.

Make a ground plan of the house and put in all the measurements of the rooms.

Draw the big wooden latch on the main door of the house.
How does it work?

Imagine there was a terrible cold gale blowing. What do you think it would be like in the house?
How would you help to make a family comfortable if they lived there in olden times?

Choose some friends and practise a recorder piece to play in the gallery when you have your next visit to the house.

Whittle some pegs to plug beams.

This one is difficult.
Weigh a piece of old timber.
Now estimate the weight of the biggest cruck. Measure it.
What kind of lorry would you suggest for transport?

List the number of materials you can find in the building.

Find a bit of soft wood.
Carve it.

Draw a map of the district. Enter any timber-framed building. Ask around to get information.

What do you think is the nicest thing about the house? Why do you like it?

How is the house constructed to counteract wind resistance?
If you don't know, look at it and see if you can work it out.

Appendix B   Greek vases in the British Museum: assignments

These assignments use the Greek vases as starting points for creative work. Selecting, copying, and photographing would all lead to greater commitment in looking. Different studies could lead to a deeper knowledge of the pots, the materials, and the techniques that were used and the social conditions under which the vases were made.

Play forgeries:
Make early Greek pots nobody has ever seen before.
When you have finished make comments on your forgeries under the two headings, Failure and Success.

Produce puppet plays of Greek myths, using rod and shadow puppets.
Get information from Greek vases.
Accompany the action with readings from the Greek myths and with improvised sound effects using simple wind instruments and drums that you have made yourselves.

Make a continuous scroll painting of music and dance from Greek pots.
Do it in the Greek idiom but with some reference to Chinese scroll paintings.
Instead of operating the scroll painting by hand as the Chinese did, work out some mechanism for unfolding and refolding more in line with modern, twentieth-century methods.

A game with Greek myths:
Draw the most improbable happening you can find on a Greek vase.
Swop yours with a friend.
Work out a new myth to suit the illustration you have acquired.
Stick this illustration on a sheet of an agreed size and, in fine, black, fibre-tipped pen, write out your Greek myth to go with it. Clip all the new myths together and decorate a cover with variants of Greek key patterns.

Athletics:
Make studies of athletic prowess from Greek pots.
Use them for posters and programmes.
    1. For your school sports.
    2. For the Olympic Games.
    3. For part of a film on sport which you can shoot in any way you like.
For script connected with these projects use a typewriter and Letraset which may be applied, traced, or drawn, adapting to size as you like.

Go round the collection of Greek vases with friends and make plans for work connected with them. Write each idea, with some indication of follow-up, on a card, so that the lot can be passed round and discussed before choices are made. The work can be carried out by individuals or groups of any size. If individuals have a strong desire to go on observing rather than to develop work, this activity is valid.

Some vases which can be seen at the British Museum

For children from Islington (high percentage of Greek children):

Discuss and record Greek food and recipes.
Scout round for information.
Imagine you were starting a Greek restaurant in Islington.
Where would you open it and how would you choose equipment, furniture, decor, etc.?
Work out restaurant sign, advertising, and menu cards using motifs from Greek pots in the British Museum.

Appendix C   Montagu Motor Museum Teaching Pack

The Southampton Curriculum Development Centre has produced a resource pack of teaching materials for older junior children and younger pupils in secondary schools. The contents of the pack evolved from the experiences of a Southampton middle school teacher when he organized a travel project based on visits to the Motor Museum.

The pack contains the following materials:

a case history outlining the original project and giving details of its organization;

a flow chart suggesting possible areas of study;

twenty-five work cards (these are offered as suggestions on which teachers might base their own assignments – they do not constitute a scheme of work);

guided tour notes to the museum;

a brief history of the motor car prepared by the museum librarian;

twenty-eight photographs of cars, accessories, motorists' clothing, early garages, etc. (these are accompanied by a cassette tape commentary);

twelve slides of veteran, vintage, and racing cars, again with a taped commentary;

a museum guide book and a picture book of old vehicles;

a Brooke Bond chart dealing with the history of the motor car;

suggested science experiments;

a bibliography and a list of film material;

ideas for linking this field of study to the Schools Council's Science 5–13 Project, with particular reference to the project's booklets *Metals* and *Structures and Forces*.

These resource packs are made available to Southampton schools by the city's Curriculum Development Centre. An inspection copy can be obtained by chief education officers of other authorities from the Chief Education Officer, Civic Centre, Southampton.

Appendix D Films: *What Do I See?* and *Insight*

Both films, *What Do I See?* (eight minutes) and *Insight* (four minutes), are an exercise in visual perception. The camera has become the eye of the expert who knows what to look for and how to look, so that the imagination is stimulated by unexpected contrasts in shape and colour.

Absence of factual information, other than identification of the objects, in *What Do I See?* is deliberate. Objects are intended to be starting points for personal discovery and interest, which will take many forms according to individual reaction.

The relatively slow tempo of the films is deliberate. Experience shows that it takes time to create a full awareness of what is seen on the screen. It is only at the first viewing, however, that the speed appears to be slow; at the second showing the images pass quickly. It is hoped that both films will be used experimentally by teachers in the classroom, by lecturers at colleges of education, and in teachers' centres.

The objects shown in *What Do I See?* are as follows:

> Neolithic stone axe head $9\frac{1}{2}$ in long
> Bronze Age clay beaker   8 in high
> Roman glass bottle   11 in high
> Roman glass beaker   5 in high
> Medieval wax Seal of Dover   4 in diameter
> thirteenth-century gilt on bronze crucifix   5 in high
> eighteenth-century lead tobacco jar   6 in high

Insight may lead to creative writing, painting, or simply to an enhanced awareness of objects.

In *What Do I See?*, which was filmed in the Lincoln City and County Museum, any one object, such as the Roman glass or the medieval bronze Christ, could awaken the desire to find out more about a particular period and could lead to new fields of study. The selection of the objects in this film was made by three individuals who chose the six things they preferred in the Lincoln Museum. The final selection attempts within this range to cover as far as possible the museum collections. It is hoped that the film will also be shown to visitors in one of the museum galleries to encourage identification with the original and to lead to further exploration of the objects. The working party felt that experiments of this kind in regional museums as well as in national museums could be of educational value to visitors in all age groups.

It has not been thought necessary to identify the shells, etc., shown in *Insight*. All the rocks and crystals were filmed at the Lincoln City and County Museum.

Joint Working Party on Museums

Mrs M. Long (Chairman)	Head of Department of Art and Design, Shenstone College of Education
H. J. Davis	Headmaster, Ynysawdre Comprehensive School, Tondu, Glamorgan
W. H. George	Headmaster, Haverstock School, Chalk Farm, London
Mrs R. Marcousé	Secretary of the International Council of Museums (ICOM) Committee for Education and Cultural Action, formerly education officer at the Victoria and Albert Museum, London
D. Moore	Senior Officer, Schools Service, National Museum of Wales, Cardiff
D. E. Powell	Headmaster, Treorchy Junior School, Rhondda, Glamorgan
A. G. Razzell	Senior Project Officer, Schools Council Middle Years of Schooling Project, University of Lancaster
H. R. Singleton	Director, Department of Museum Studies, University of Leicester
W. W. Taylor	HM Inspector with responsibility for Museums
D. E. Turner	Principal, Cardiff College of Art, formerly Head of Department of Foundation Studies, Lanchester Polytechnic, Coventry
J. W. Watts	Headmaster, Hurstmere Secondary Boys' School, Sidcup, Kent
R. D. Price (Secretary)	Curriculum Officer, Schools Council